COMMUNICATION IN MARRIAGE

*20 Golden Rules
Behind an Extraordinary
Marriage*

SIMON GRANT

© Copyright 2019 by Simon Grant - All rights reserved.

This document is geared towards providing exact and reliable information in regards to the topic and issue covered. The publication is sold with the idea that the publisher is not required to render accounting, officially permitted, or otherwise, qualified services. If advice is necessary, legal or professional, a practiced individual in the profession should be ordered.

- From a Declaration of Principles which was accepted and approved equally by a Committee of the American Bar Association and a Committee of Publishers and Associations.

In no way is it legal to reproduce, duplicate, or transmit any part of this document in either electronic means or in printed format. Recording of this publication is strictly prohibited and any storage of this document is not allowed unless with written permission from the publisher. All rights reserved.

The information provided herein is stated to be truthful and consistent, in that any liability, in terms of inattention or otherwise, by any usage or abuse of any policies, processes, or directions contained within is the solitary and utter responsibility of the recipient reader. Under no circumstances will any legal responsibility or blame be held against the publisher for any reparation, damages, or monetary loss due to the information herein, either directly or indirectly.

Respective authors own all copyrights not held by the publisher.

The information herein is offered for informational purposes solely and is universal as so. The presentation of the information is without a contract or any type of guarantee assurance.

The trademarks that are used are without any consent, and the publication of the trademark is without permission or backing by the trademark owner. All trademarks and brands within this book are for clarifying purposes only and are owned by the owners themselves, not affiliated with this document.

Table of Contents

Introduction 1

Chapter One: RULE NO. 1
- PRIORITIZE COMMUNICATION 4
    Communication challenges couples face 7
    Simple communication techniques 9
    KEY POINTS 12

Chapter Two: RULE NO. 2
- CULTIVATE GENUINE LOVE FOR YOUR PARTNER 13
    ATTRACTION VS INFATUATION VS TRUE LOVE 14
    True Love 17
    Cultivating Love 18
    The four types of love explained 19
    KEY POINTS 20

Chapter Three: RULE NO. 3
- SHOW PROPER RESPECT 21
    Earn your Respect 24
    KEY POINTS 26

Chapter Four: RULE NO. 4
- THE VALUE OF COMMITMENT 27
    Strengthening your commitment 29
    KEY POINTS 32

Chapter Five: RULES NOS. 5 & 6
- FORGIVENESS AND REPENTANCE 33
    Forgiveness 33
    Benefits of Forgiveness in Marriage 36
    REPENTANCE 38
    The Dangers of Pride 39
    Signs of a sincere Repentance 39
    KEY POINTS 41

Chapter Six: RULE NO. 7
- THE VALUE OF TRUST 42
    Three reasons why you need trust in your marriage 43
    Building and Rebuilding Trust in your Marriage 45
    Communication 46
    Transparency 47
    Project: 47

Chapter Seven: RULE NO. 8
- AVOID RESENTMENT 49
    Resentment Signals 50
    How to prevent a prolonged resentment 52
    Key Points 54

Chapter Eight: RULE NO. 9
- PROPER VIEW OF SEXUAL INTIMACY 55
Principle of mutual Agreement 56
Tips for Improving Your Sex Lives 57
Make do with what you have 57
Learn the art of a 'Quickie 58
Don't be so boring 58
Communicate 59

Chapter Nine: RULE NO. 10
– HONESTY 60
How the Dangers of Dishonesty 61
Dangers of Dishonesty 63
Conquering Dishonesty 64
RULE NO. 11- PATIENCE 64
Dangers 65
Cultivating Patience 66

Chapter Ten: RULE NO. 12
- SPEND TIME WITH EACH OTHER 68
Reasons you should think more about spending time together 68
How to make time for your spouse 69
Enjoy a relaxing moment 71
Eat out 72
Go to the Cinema 72
Take a walk once in a while 73

Plan Romantic Nights 73
Include it in your plans 73
RULE NO. 13- COOPERATION/TEAMWORK 74
KEY POINTS 79

Chapter Eleven: RULE NO. 14
- CONTROL YOUR ANGER 80
Common causes of anger 80
RULE NO. 15- BE FLEXIBLE WITH FINANCES 85

Chapter Twelve: RULE NO. 16
- BE HARDWORKING 91
Responsibilities 91
Communication 92
Forgiveness 93
Staying Faithful 94
Benefits of hard work in a marriage 94
RULE NO. 17- KINDNESS 96
How to conquer hurtful speeches 107
Imitate Exemplary Couples 107
Rekindle Your Feelings 107
Know when to stop 108

Chapter Thirteen: RULE NO. 18
- SELF-CONTROL 109
Strengthening Your Self-Control 110
RULE NO. 19- BE PEACEABLE 110
Tips to becoming Peaceful 113

GET HELP- 118

RULE NO. 20- PROPER VIEW OF PARENTING 118

How to Reason on Child Limits... 119

Mutually agree on consequences 120

Have each other's back 120

Never Argue in front of your children over the rules............. 121

Be Adaptable 121

KEY POINTS 121

Conclusion **123**

References **125**

Introduction

Marriage between a man and a woman is supposed to be a lifelong union. However, this union is under attack in several places across the globe. Consider the United States for example: according to a recent survey of marriages, almost 50% of first marriages will end in divorce. That rate is even higher if one or both parties have been married before.

In the United Kingdom, the survey found out almost the same thing, with some 45% of new marriages believed to be heading for divorce. Worse still, about 20% of these divorces happen between 1-3 years of marriage, while some marriages sadly end after a few months. Looking at this trend spread from one country to another is really sickening considering the human natural tendency of being loved.

When finding out some of the reasons for divorce in these situations, financial issues ranks number one. Other reasons may include infidelity of one or both parties, different views of marital intimacy, emotional strain, lack of communication, lack of real love for each other, among others.

When these issues come up, many quickly forget that beautiful day that the words "I DO" were the best two-lettered word in the whole universe. They quickly forget the marital vows they took that made clear their determination to stay together through thick and thin, till death comes along. According to that marriage vows, only death should put an end to their union together as husband and wife.

On the other hand, there are couples that have lived together for years. An example is Mr. and Mrs. William (names have been changed) have lived together in the United States for over 60 years as husband and wife. They were interviewed and asked what the key to the success of their union was. They both agreed that even though living together as a couple is not easy, they have learned to show true love and respect in their marriage.

So, true marital success lies not in the institution- marriage, but with the people involved. A lack of commitment is ever more on the rise with people have stopped treating the marital arrangement as sacred. They allow work, as well as other mundane things, jeopardize their love and respect for their marriage mates, while the allure of extramarital affairs is also on the rise. So, what really can be done to salvage this rather ugly, downhill trend of modern marriages?

Marriage can be compared to a well-prepared meal that has all the necessary ingredients for a sumptuous taste. When one ingredient is absent, it reflects how the meal will taste. So, for a marriage to be successful, it must have all the necessary ingredients that will help the couple live together happily, and in peace. These ingredients are nothing but the beautiful qualities that a husband and wife need to cultivate for their marriage to continue thriving.

They say the first year of marriage is always tough on both parties involved. Even tougher a period is when problems start plaguing the union.

This book does not claim to have all the answers as no two marriages are the same. However, therein lie basic guidelines for a successful relationship between married couples. You will also find useful suggestions that a husband or wife can follow in certain common situations that couples face today. You will also be glad to read some comments made by older couples on what has helped them stay true to one another for so long.

By the time you complete this exciting and engaging book, you can be confident that you have found the key to a successful marital life.

Chapter One

RULE NO. 1- PRIORITIZE COMMUNICATION

For a relationship to thrive there must be effective communication between those involved. It is a way of conveying your innermost concerns, thoughts, and desires with a view to understanding each other better. However, most relationship today starts to falter the moment this vital ingredient to a successful marriage is neglected.

Communication is a two-way thing- speaking and listening. So a husband and wife should create time to be with each other so that they can both express themselves as well as listen to the feelings of the other person. For communication to be effective, it must be done with a desire to please the other person. It is no longer an effective communication if all we do is shout at the top of our voices or even start lying blames on the other party.

So what can you really do to improve your communication skills with your spouse? What should you avoid if you want your marriage to be successful? Well, let us consider a few.

Don't be too quick to anger- Granted, there might be occasions when tempers might flare-up. This is because we all make mistakes in speech from time to time. If we allow tempers to flare up too easily, constructive communication can easily turn ugly. So, when you notice that you are starting to get frustrated by what your partner is saying, take some time to breathe in and out. Think about how you want your relationship to be like, and then really listen to what your spouse is saying.

This way, you will not allow a simple conversation to turn to a wildfire of arguments. The truth is that anger can easily reduce the amount of meaningful conversation you should be having as a couple. So, every time you and your spouse decide to talk about how you both feel, be calm and gentle with your words. You will be surprised how much respect your spouse will have for you. You never can tell. You might just be teaching your spouse what good communication should look like by your fine example.

Avoid apportioning blames- It is true that when an issue comes up, one person is usually the cause. In other common cases, both parties might be responsible for the strain in the relationship. So, if you will ever sit down to talk about the situation, learn to always point out where you when wrong, instead of always pointing out the faults of your spouse. If your spouse will be at peace with you, they must be convinced that you always tolerate them and no always criticize them.

If on the other hand, you are in the habit of always apportioning blames, then before long, your partner will be tired of having a simple conversation with you. Even if it is really glaring that you partner is at fault, why not allow him or her to mention and apologize for it instead of using their fault as a weapon to win the argument? This will give them freeness of speech with you.

Listen to how you sound- it is very easy to see the faults in other people's manner of conversation. However, no one really sees their own faults except when alerted to it. So try this: the next time you and your spouse are discussing, try to listen to yourself and how you sound. Try to understand the words coming out of your mouth, and see if there are no implied meanings to them. You might be surprised to find out that unbeknownst to you, you were quite rude when expressing yourself.

If you notice that there is something you should work on in the way you converse with your spouse, do not delay in correcting it. The effort is well worth it as you will improve the manner of conversation with your spouse. Your spouse will feel more relaxed in expressing their thoughts and concerns. You will become their best friend and nothing will be able to separate you both.

Discuss problems before they escalate- If not attended to promptly, unresolved differences can build up to the extent that they hinder you both from cooperating with each other. So, when you notice a change in your spouse' reactions, that is the best time to talk it out. Remember that the aim is not to win the argument. You want to make up with them and make them happy again. So, listen to their concern(s) and calmly accept responsibility for any part you played in the issue. When you make it a point of duty to always say "I'm sorry", you will become very much skilled at resolving the occasional differences you might have with your partner through meaningful communication.

Communication challenges couples face

- **Busy lifestyles-** In today's rush hour life, couples spend less time with each other and this can sometimes affect how much conversations they have daily. In some parts of the world, when they both leave for work very early in the day, they will only return home tired late at night. Getting home will be all about having dinner and sleeping off. This has created a communication gap between the two of them.

- **Negative body language-** body languages involve facial expression, gestures, and eyes rolling. When a spouse notices this in his or her partner, it can act as a deterrent to good and meaningful communication.

- **Playing the blame game-** As earlier mentioned, this is another reason some couples don't communicate at all today. No one wants to always wake up to their faults being thrown right at their face. When a husband is always blaming the wife for every mistake at home, this can always discourage the wife from creating time and really expressing herself to her husband.

- **Humiliating your spouse-** we speak every day, some positive while others are negative. When you fall into the habit of always tearing down your spouse with hurtful speech, maybe degrading her because of where she comes from or because of her race or family background, we are indirectly making them uneasy around us, which can eventually increase the gap of communication between us.

- **Keeping an account of injuries-** sometimes, it is just best to let bygones be bygones. We are all imperfect which means we make mistakes every day. It also translates to means that couple will keep hurting each other in little ways as long as they both live together. So, when past mistakes are always brought to the fore every time couple discusses, it will only discourage the other party from having a good conversation.

- **Arguments-** forget what you watch in movies, marriage is not a game to determine who is better at shouting out his points more. There is more wisdom in calmly discussing differences than always raising voices. If arguments are habitual, communication will definitely be affected negatively between the couple.

- **Thoughtless speech-** sometimes, we say things that we don't really mean. This may be because we didn't really give careful thoughts to the words we speak. Often times, when we speak this way, we only hurt others. When someone's feelings are hurt, most times they only withdraw to their emotional shell and communication is the least they worry about.

- **Not really Listening-** You will agree that speaking with someone who does not listen to us is nothing but futile. The same is true of a marriage today when one spouse hardly listens to the other; the hurt spouse will automatically find no pleasure in divulging their feelings to them anymore. In such marriages, communication may be nothing but perfunctory.

Simple communication techniques

With the problems highlighted above, here are some sure techniques to help bridge the gap of communication between marriage mates. As you read through them, try and imagine how your marital life will be when applied. They are suggestions that are sure to work as offered by some older couples who have spent years in marriage.

1. **Learn to be quiet when your mate is speaking-** two of you cannot both talk at the same time. So, when they speak, make sure you are not just quiet but actually listen to what they have to say. Playing with your smartphone while she expresses herself is really not the way out. Watching the TV while she's pouring out her feelings too isn't the best thing to you. When you take your time to listen while she speaks, she will also be impelled to listen to you whenever you want to express yourself.

2. **Give careful thought to your words-** In marriage, your partner will no doubt give your promises or insults more attention than the ones they hear from someone other than their spouses. So if your conversation must be meaningful, it

is imperative that you think well before you speak. You may have the right intentions but if you do not convey them the right way, you may only be adding fuel to the issue on ground. Remember, you are talking to your husband or wife, so choose your words carefully.

3. **Understand that their point of view may be different-** Whenever you are to discuss an important issue, always remember that you are not always right. Even if you are the head of the family, which does not automatically grant you a veto power to become a monarch at home, always imposing your own view. Listen to your spouse, try and see things their way, and if you can make allowances for it, her suggestions can be implemented once in a while. This way she will feel valued and will actively take part in subsequent conversations.

4. **Observe their body language-** simple things like the rolling of eyes or some other simple gestures might suggest that your partner isn't happy about something. So even though they are not saying anything, you can discern what is in their heart by observing their body language when you say something or make a certain decision. They might not want to utter those words but only a discerning mate will make an effort to understand those unsaid words. For example, if your husband or wife is giving you a silent treatment at home, it is an indication of something you didn't say or do right. Kindly

call out your partner calmly and discuss it? You may be surprised at what good this will do to your marriage.

5. **Be honest-** when conveying your thoughts to your spouse, be sincere with them and always make sure you do not tell lies. Telling lies will only require more lies to cover up. And the more lies you tell, the more you weaken their trust in your statements. So, even if your spouse might get angry, it is always good to speak the truth. They will forever remember you for that and will never have any cause to doubt your statements.

6. **Limit third party interference-** if you want to improve the level of communication between you and your spouse, avoid the trap of always bringing in a third party to solve your issues for you. Communication in the marital arrangement should be between you and your spouse and not between you, your spouse and your relatives.

So, as we have seen effective communication can really help you both strengthen the bond between you as a couple. It is true that the world we live in today prides phone conversations as the easiest way out. While that is not a bad idea, it should never replace physical conversation. You will never get to read a person's body language over the internet via a phone call.

Make time for a meaningful conversation between you and your spouse and watch how much his will impact on your marriage. In the next chapter, we will discuss the second rule for a successful marriage- cultivating a genuine love for your partner.

KEY POINTS
- If you want a successful marriage, you must make time to communicate with your spouse

- Arguments, dishonesty, apportioning blames, and a busy lifestyle are just some deterrents to a meaningful conversation between couples today

- Always learn to listen to the unspoken words when you are communicating with your partner. This can be done by observing their body language

Chapter Two

RULE NO. 2- CULTIVATE GENUINE LOVE FOR YOUR PARTNER

Love, that word has often been misused or even misunderstood over the years. For a marriage to be successful, the husband and the wife involved must really love each other. But love, genuine love is not a product of chance. It is something that must be cultivated. And sometimes it may take time for two people to really love each other that way.

Love is the feeling we have when we are deeply affectionate about someone. As humans, we all want to feel loved, so is your husband or wife. It is just as William Shakespeare describes it that "absence from those we love is self from self-a deadly banishment." Feeling loved is like a sure medicine for the most painful ailments in a marriage. But in the world we live in today, true love has proved elusive for many people, even for some married couples.

Well, the problem is that many people confuse true love with infatuation. So before we continue on the subject of cultivating true love, let us quickly understand the difference between love and infatuation. Then we will consider the four different types of love and how you can cultivate them in your marriage.

ATTRACTION VS INFATUATION VS TRUE LOVE

True love should be the foundation of any marriage for that marital institution to be successful. However, many people today because of mere attraction or infatuation.

The attraction is based on what you see that catches your attention. A young woman may be attractive because of how she dresses or because of her nice smile whenever she makes eye contact. Well, who among us isn't attracted to a beautiful lady or a handsome young man that walks around confidently? We are not just attracted, but we admire them and want to be friends with them.

Some people quickly equate this to true love, thus basing their marriage on this fickle foundation. No wonder it is popular today to hear such things as 'Love at first sight'. Love, at first sight, is nothing but attraction. They forget that attraction only has to do with what is obvious to the human eyes and as such, marriages found on this foundation are already heading for its end. Simply said, such marriages don't last long.

Infatuation, on the other hand, is a step above mere attraction because it involves little but a short-lived passion. Infatuation too is quite strong a feeling, but such attachment is termed an 'unreasonable' one. This is because infatuation is blind, just as it is mistaken for love today by such statements as 'Love is blind'. Infatuation will see obvious reasons why two people cannot be marriage mates but will rate the passion above the obvious differences.

For example, imagine a man and a woman who met in a nightclub and were easily attracted to each other. Well, after a few dates they decided to get married. While close to the marriage- all in the space of three months- the lady discovered that the guy smokes, drinks, and is abusive. But she keeps convincing herself that her love should be able to overlook those vices even though she finds them very irritating. That is infatuation; it blinds the eye of someone to the truth all in the name of passion.

Infatuation is deadly because it is deceitful and is the cause of many divorces today. When the couples finally tie the marital knots, they find that the passion fades off sooner than they expected. They dawn on them the reality- all the irritating things now start coming to the fore and before you know it, they go their separate ways.

Note the difference between infatuation and real love. Infatuation is always selfish and self-centered. Always making the person thinking about him and what benefits them first before thing about the other person. Real love, as you will come to understand is not blind and is never selfish.

How can you know if it is really infatuation? Ask yourself what is most important to your partner, and if you don't come in the top 3, then know that your bond is only built on a flimsy ground as infatuation. With infatuation, you always hear things like "no one makes **me** feel good like you", "what you plan to do won't really suit **me**", "**I** will be happy if you could do…." You notice that the words "**me**" or "**I**" take priority in everything said and done. So when they get married, as soon as they don't get what they want, then little problems will make them abandon the ship for another ship so to speak.

Consider these clear signals of infatuation

- It thinks selfishly almost all the time, thinking, "What benefit will I get?"

- Romance starts almost immediately after meeting (maybe hours), and it happens almost every time they see

- Only appreciates the obvious in their partner- especially physical appearance

- Makes someone blind to the imperfections of their mate

- Occasional arguments, most times settle over sexual intercourse

- Makes you act strange even discarding useful advice from well-meaning family members

The fact remains that any relationship that is built on infatuation will never be happy nor will it be successful. For a marriage to be successful, it must be built on true love for one another. So, what is true love?

True Love

Have you ever taken note of how some marriages stand the tests of time? Even though serious problems they never seem to falter? What does that suggest to you? Yes, that marriage was built on something more than a mere attraction or infatuation. It is a strong feeling of attachment that is not blind to the imperfections of one another. Instead of focusing on **me** or **I**, such a relationship puts **you** and **we** to the fore.

Well, some might argue that infatuation and love are not different. The truth is they are different because true love is based on what you know about the person; it has little to do with the physical appearance. As the years roll by, you will find out that you still feel strongly about that person. This is because the foundation of true love is not transient but something that lasts forever. Even if the body fades, the character remains the same and so does the feelings.

How can you know if it is true love? It is evident in what your partner says about the reason they want to be with you. It is also evident in how he treats other people related to you, like your family members and friends. What is their reaction when you give a suggestion or a viewpoint? Is your spouse all about physical intimacy and sex? Also, consider what they say about you behind your back. If they really love you they will never put you down in the presence of others. How do they react when you make mistakes?

Remember that infatuation is blind but true love is not. How so? When it is infatuation, the person's mistakes will always be played down because of the passion. But that's not the case with true love. True love sees the imperfections of the other person clearly. True love recognizes that nobody is perfect and that we all have our good sides as well as our bad sides. True love will try to compare someone's good sides as well as bad sides. So, a person who truly loves you will never expect perfection from you after marriage. They are well aware of your weaknesses and are determined to love you in spite of those weaknesses.

Have you ever heard people say, "time will tell"? Well, if you want to know if someone really loves you, allow your emotions to endure the test of time. If after many months or a few years they still feel the same about you, then it is likely real love that they have for you. Now if you are a dating couple and you want a successful marriage, this might be easier to do- allowing time to pass before really committing your emotions. But what if you are already married? The best thing is to start cultivating true love for the person you are married to.

Cultivating Love

- Learn to be unselfish in how you treat your husband or wife. Be determined to always place their interests ahead of your own

- Don't be too enthusiastic about sexual intimacy. Allow something else other than sex to be the thing that draws you closer to the person

- Spend quality time in communicating with them. Share your feelings without prompt, your goals and desires.

- Write down a list of the things you don't like about them, as well as a list of what you like about them. In most cases, the second list is longer than the first. Learn to appreciate their good qualities more than their negative traits. Commend your spouse for something they do that you appreciate daily.

- Avoid always reporting your spouse to their family members and friends. Also, avoid belittling them before your own close family members. This will only jeopardize your bond.

- Make sure you discuss issues that you have amicably without many arguments. Instead of shouting, practice expressing yourself without raising your voice.

The four types of love explained

In the ancient Greek language, the English word 'Love' can be rendered in four different ways. They all differ slightly but must all be understood if you are to show love to your marriage mate.

Agape- a form of love that is evident in the actions that it prompts. It is a type of love that is selfless and put other people's interest ahead of the one who displays it. It is not the love for affection and intimacy that this denotes as it is only shown in actions. It is indeed a type of love that is guided by principles.

Stor-ge- a type of affection that exists between family members

Phi-li'a - love or affection between friends of the same sex or different sexes

E'ros- this is the romantic affection that exists between lovers as well as husband or wife

Considering the above-mentioned types of love, which of them is really important if your marriage is to be successful? They are all vital because your mate is supposed to be your best friend as well as your closest family member. So, since agape encompasses all of them, then agape love, a love based on principle is the most important one.

In the next chapter, we will learn of the third rule for a successful marriage- Respect.

KEY POINTS

- Attraction and Infatuation is really different from Love

- The best kind of love is the principled, self-sacrificing love which will make your marriage a success

- The four kinds of love are EROS, AGAPE, STORGE, and PHILIA. They are all important if your marriage must be successful.

Chapter Three

RULE NO. 3 - SHOW PROPER RESPECT

Simply put if you respect someone, you will honor and show them consideration. If you are a husband or a wife, you must learn to always show consideration to your spouse, which will eventually do much in solidifying the bond between you both. Respect in your relationship will contribute immensely to the joy and success of your marriage.

Because you respect your spouse, you don't feel burdened in assigning them a bit of dignity even though you are the head of your family. This dignity is evident in kind words and actions. Even if they need something, respect motivates you to want to do it for them. Now let us look at two important areas where is really important to show respect for your mate. For someone who truly respects his or her marriage mate, their partner is always their priority. So, when they want to choose a form of recreation, for example, they recognize that it is not always about them but what the other person likes as well. The same principle will apply in the choice of music when traveling together in a car or when shopping. It can even apply when it comes to the choice of meals.

Some people always think that only the wife should respect her husband. But as the definition puts it, it means showing each other consideration. So, as much as the wife is expected to respect the decisions of the husband, the husband too, on the other hand, must respect his wife's wishes and should show her more than enough consideration.

Choices- Respect will help you remember that you are not always right, or that what you like may not be appealing to another person. Take for example the matter of child-rearing. A woman may want a specific number of kids while her husband's choice may be to remain childless. In other cases, it is the wife that may not want children while the husband, in this case, may want children. If not properly handled, this can cause a lot of problems in the marital arrangement. They need to respect each other choices and 'meet each other halfway' so to speak.

Another area where marriage mates need to respect each other's choices is handling personal problems. Sometimes, respecting other people's choices might mean accepting that you can't decide for them. In some developing countries, a husband always feels like he can command the wife around as he feels like. Even though it is the norm in such places, it doesn't mean it is the right thing to do. For marriage mates to live happily, they should be free to make certain decisions on their own. No one wants to be imprisoned in their own house.

Speech- We will always talk about people, even to/ about our spouses. Remember the definition of respect we gave earlier? It involves giving consideration to someone and how they feel. When couples speak with each other, they need to show respect to one another. Abusive speech and hateful comments should have no place in a marital arrangement. Even if one of them has made a serious error in judgment, it is still no reason to start hurling insults at each other. A calm reply can defuse an angry reaction at times, so respect your spouse, respect your marriage and do not let little things start making your speak disrespectfully to your partner.

What about when speaking with others like close family members and friends about your partner? Still, if you want your marriage to be as strong as ever, you must always show by what you say about your spouse that you respect her. When you are with your friends, if you call your husband a "moron", it is most likely that your friends will start viewing your husband as one. Or what if you label your wife a "fool"? The next time your friends want to address your wife they might start taking her as a fool. So, speak well of your marriage mate such that when they hear what you said about them behind their back, it will definitely contribute much to the respect in your union.

Be careful not to reveal things shared with you in secrecy with people, even other family members. Your husband trusts you and that is why he told you about that contract at work. It would be utterly disrespectful if he finds out that you had divulged such information to your friends or even in-laws. Respect confidentiality and keep the information secret until they want to let it out.

Earn your Respect

Respect is not something to be demanded, it can only be earned. What you do, how you do them, what you say, and how you say them will all contribute to whether your husband or wife will respect you or not.

As you all know, a husband is the head of the family. This means that he takes the lead in providing food, shelter, and clothing for the family. Apart from that, he must be selfless in providing for the family. But what will happen if a husband fails to provide for the family? What if he becomes lazy and let the wife start taking care of the family's physical needs? Definitely, the wife will never give him as much respect as he would have expected. But if he takes seriously his responsibility of being the family head, never allowing his family lack anything good, then he will never need to ask his wife to respect him but he will have earned it through his actions.

Another area where a husband needs to earn his respect is in his use of authority. The atmosphere at home should be a relaxed one where the wife can feel the freedom that comes from marriage. But what do you think will happen if a husband starts misusing his authority, overly restricting his wife in actions and movements? What if the husband writes down a list of dos and don'ts for the wife, commanding her every move? Surely the wife will have little respect for such a husband. But when you let her do some things on her own, maybe making some home-bound decisions, you as a husband, are only earning your respect little by little. If you want your wife to respect you as a husband, treat her well, show loving consideration for her needs, and you will enjoy her support always.

There are times during the month that a woman may feel weak and cannot perform some of her duties at home. It could be an occasional mood swing, or she could be on her monthly cycle. There is nothing stopping the husband from helping her out with those chores. What about sex? Don't always pressure your woman to have sex with you especially during these times. Show understanding of her current situation and deal with her in like manner. You will be surprised by how much respect your wife will give to you.

A wife too can earn the respect of her husband if she strives to be a supportive wife. A wife's place is not to question every of her husband's movements and decisions. Truth be said, there is a measure of jealousy in every healthy marital relationship, but when she makes it her aim to always monitor her husband's movements, mobile devices, and so on, she is really belittling herself before the husband.

There are times that a man's emotions may be down. This could be because of a problem at home, or at work. It could be an occasional mood swing or he could just have remembered something that made him sad. During those times, a wife that wants to earn her husband's respect will let her husband be by not troubling him with other unnecessary things at that moment.

A wife who takes as serious her responsibility at home will only gain more respect from her husband. No one likes a lazy wife, and no one wants a wife who can't cook. So, if you want to earn the respect of your husband, be a worker at home, do laundry the when due, cook instead of wasting the household income on junks, and pay attention to your kids is you are raising a child. You will have earned the respect of your man. Next, we will consider another rule that can help marriage mates be successful- Commitment.

KEY POINTS

- Respecting your spouse will help your marriage be successful
- Both the man and the woman can show respect in the marriage
- Respect must not be demanded, it can only be earned.

Chapter Four

RULE NO. 4- THE VALUE OF COMMITMENT

The wedding day will long be remembered for the elegance and the nice dresses worn by the couple. It will also be remembered for the way that day brought together family and friends from way back. But one thing should make the day special for the couple- the vows taken. That solemn promise showed that you both are determined to spend the rest of your lives with each other.

That promise made is supposed to be a lifelong commitment. It is like making a strong resolve that come what may, no matter the problems encountered along the way, you will stick with your marriage mate. But as the years roll by, emotions get strained by various problems. Unpleasant circumstances, family members and in-laws get in the way, and more crucial that handsome and beautiful face begins to age. Will you still feel that same devotion you felt on your wedding day?

Consider this real-life scenario:

A man named Jacques who has been married to his wife for 10 years started noticing that his wife was no longer close to him emotionally. After much suspicion of what could be the problem, he picked up her phone one night only to go through her messages and notice that some strange man and his wife had been exchanging messages. He went further only to find out that the man was her workmate. He felt so bad and started to cry.

What do you think was the problem in their relationship? Granted they didn't start the marriage on that note. So what changed? Was the co-worker showing a romantic interest at work the problem? The answer is no. the romantic interest is just a symptom. The real issue is a lack of commitment.

So, if you too feel the relationship between you and your wife have weakened over the years, the problem may be a commitment in the marriage. So what exactly is a commitment?

It is like a dedication or pledge to someone or something, which in this case is your spouse. Remember the vows you took on your wedding day? You promised to stay in the marriage no matter what. It is like saying no matter what happens we will always work it out. Little wonder why some use the term "loyalty" in describing commitment between couples.

Commitment should not be done out of a sense of duty, as this could easily become boring and lack real purpose. Some marriage mates stay committed to their wives because of the children they have together. That too isn't a good reason to stay committed in a marriage. The marriage bond should bring joy to those involved. Contentment should be evident in the faces of marriage mates. They should learn to trust each other and become each other's friends. In fact, they must be best friends with each other. They should also learn to do things together, like go on vacations, do house chores, and even drive to work together if they work along the same axis. As they do all of these together, they will be more committed to their marriage, loyal to each other, and will be better equipped to withstand the wear and tear of time on their bond.

Commitment is the force that drives marriages through thick and thin. When you are committed to your marriage, even if you fight and argue and say all sorts of things to each other, you are confident that neither of you is abandoning the marriage. In the end, you will talk it out with your spouse. You are sure that the marriage is steady and going nowhere, thus you are poised to discuss the misunderstanding in the long run with your spouse.

Are you having a lot of issues in your marriage? Will you like to end this negative trend? The answer is to strengthen the commitment to your marriage.

Strengthening your commitment
- Cultivate a healthy view of your marriage by not always feeling trapped in the union. Some people are appalled that they will be with the same person for the rest of their lives. Instead of seeing your union as a trap, view it as a sense of responsibility that it is. Remember, marriage is meant to be permanent and not a ship that you jump out once you notice a problem.

- Avoid threatening your spouse by leaving every time you have a disagreement. Doing this will only undermine your marriage and will not make them happy at all. In the heat of arguments, we are prone to saying things that we might regret later.

- Be determined to make your marriage work. Even if you were raised in a divided household, or even if your parents divorced, make a concerted effort never to allow your marriage to be like theirs.

- Make sure that your priority lies with your marriage. Ask yourself how important is your marriage to you the answer to this question will reveal if you are really committed to your marriage or not. Make sure to regularly spend time with your mate. The amount of time you invest in your marriage will determine how committed you are to the marriage. On the other hand, ask your mate if they feel you are committed to the marriage. If your marriage mate thinks that you are not doing enough, don't feel embarrassed or guilty. Ask them what practical things they feel you can do in other to start showing the right kind of commitment.

- Be determined to stay loyal to your mate. Marital infidelity might be painted in the media as harmless, but the truth is that it can ruin an entire marriage. It can break trust, render children homeless, and can leave you with a strong feeling of guilt. One thing you can do is to vow never to view pornography. Imagine how your mate will feel if they find out that you are. Some couples make the mistake of viewing pornography together as a couple, thinking that it will help them spice up their sex life. But experiences have shown that it is only undermining the relationship between both of them. If there is something you want to be improved sexually, why not talk to your partner about it instead of viewing pornography.

- At work, you can send a clear signal to potential predators by placing the picture of your spouse on your desk. You can also make it an aim to always wear your wedding ring wherever you go. This will alert members of the opposite sex to the fact that you are not available.

- Do things that you both enjoy together before marriage. It could be that before marriage you both enjoy going to the movies, vacationing, mountain climbing, or even biking together. Why not engage in such activities again and see how much fun you will both have. Other ways you can rekindle your commitment is by looking at the photographs of your wedding ceremony and reliving those moments. If you have the entire wedding in video format, why not get yourself some ice cream or popcorn and watch the video together. You just might be reminded of how much you both mean to each other.

- Make a habit of always talking to your spouse about your day before you sleep. So many things had happened during the day, so many ups and downs. Your spouse is waiting for you at home and they are sure to listen. No doubt when you have shared how your day went, they too will be prompted to share their own day as well. As you both make it a habit to do this, you will be drawn together the more, and you will find out that with each passing day, your bond is getting stronger and stronger.

- Make sure you listen whenever your mate is talking to you. It will reassure them that you view them as important as the day they got married to you.

In all, if you want your marriage to be successful, you must be committed to the marriage. In the next chapter, we will examine two other antidotes to a happy marriage.

KEY POINTS

- Commitment is the force that drives marriages to success

- Loyalty is another word used in place of commitment

- Distance yourself from marital infidelity and pornography is you want to stay committed to your marriage

Chapter 5

RULES NOS. 5 & 6- FORGIVENESS AND REPENTANCE

Forgiveness

- Nobody is perfect; we can all make mistakes at times. In terms of gravity, mistakes differ. Breaking a plate might be different from kissing another man. The same way not opening the car door for your wife might be totally different from sending a suggestive text message to another woman. So, whether it is a mere argument over something that happened or something else, no matter the gravity of the mistake, is forgiveness really feasible? If you want your marriage to remain strong, you need to learn the art of forgiveness.
- No marriage is perfect, and that means every marriage has its fair share of hurts and conflicts. So don't think that only your marriage is faulty. When you forgive your marriage mate, you are letting go of what happened and the hurt they caused you without any plan to retaliate or hold them accountable for it. When couples fight and quarrel, it is all too common for them to bring up the past and start mentioning what one did months ago. If you have really forgiven your spouse, then the issue would not be brought up again in the future.

- Forgiveness is one of the building blocks of a successful marriage as it allows them to live together happily. Older couples that have lived for many decades together attest to it that offending your mate s something that will continue for as long as you both are living together. Keeping a mental ledger of pasts hurts can jeopardize your relationship if you are not careful. Many marriage mates still find it hard to forgive their mates because of some reasons.
  - **Disappointment-** when thinking about getting married, some people think that marriage will be a bed of roses without any hitch whatsoever. However, when they get married, they find out that reality is quite different from fantasy. They may have imagined a fancy house, a nice car, and the best shopping spree. But when they start struggling after marriage, they may hold their husbands for it and pick up on every little mistake he makes.
  - **Resentment-** Wounds can take some time to heal. The same is true of emotional wounds as well. When hurt all too often, some marriage mates might find it hard to let go of some hurt feelings. They might even be nurturing a desire to retaliate when the opportunity shows itself.
  - **Advantage-** Some people like to hold some form of advantage over their spouse, having them at their mercy. They might be holding off forgiveness when their spouse offends then, perhaps using it as leverage in a case where they make a serious mistake. When such happens, they will easily

refer to what the person did weeks ago and so they will not be held accountable.

- ➢ **Overthinking-** Naturally, some people think too much, and too far. They might tell their spouse that they have forgiven them, but then they go and after much thought, they relive the hurt again and again in their minds. It is like opening the emotional wounds all over again. This time they nurture fresh resentment against the person and they are not able to let go of what has happened.
- ➢ **A build-up of unresolved differences-** when issues are not resolved immediately, it becomes a little bit difficult when it is left for later. When these unresolved issues are now allowed to build up or accumulate, they can gradually lead to a stage where it becomes hard for the victim to extend forgiveness.

When allowed to foster an unwillingness to forgive can actually make two happy couples withdraw, each to their own shell so to speak. They now become cold to each other and inattentive to each other's feelings. Before you know what is going on, a once happy marriage can easily turn to an unhappy and loveless marriage.

For some others, they might claim to forgive the erring spouse but utter statements like "…..but I will never forget". So, they get pissed at the slightest of provocation by that erring mate. It is still a lack of forgiveness.

One thing that will help a couple forgive more often is to understand the benefits that come from forgiveness and how it can contribute to the success of their marriage.

Benefits of Forgiveness in Marriage

- **Peace of mind-** when you forgive your husband or wife of something they've said or done, it gives you peace of mind in the home. More often than not we hurt ourselves in the process of trying to react to something that is offensive. When we set our eyes of them, we get angry over and over and over again. You both live in the same house, which means you will keep seeing each other daily. If you don't forgive them for the error, you will find out eventually that they have more peace of mind than you. So when your spouse apologizes for what they did, kindly let it go.
- **Forgiveness strengthens your marriage-** either you like it or not, forgiveness is love. Without it, marriage will hit the rock in a matter of months. Couples fight weekly, if not daily for some. And when your spouse offends you, it will hurt you more than any other person will ever do. So, forgiveness is something that you need to keep doing if you want your love to stand the tests of time. Every time you extend forgiveness to your spouse, mention what they can do to make things better the next time so they don't keep repeating the same mistakes over and over again.
- **Helps you to be objective-** extending forgiveness will only help you handle future disagreements with much ease. When

you think about what forgiveness really involves you will figure this truth out. Before you extend forgiveness, you must have given careful thought to what could have prompted your mate to behave that way. While thinking about it you find out about the stressful day at work that very day, thus concluding that they were under some form of pressure that day. You took note of all surrounding circumstances and decided to extend forgiveness. Well, that is a good start. You have this learned that when future disagreements or misunderstanding occurs, you need to take a lot of factors into consideration. Because you extended forgiveness, you are now better equipped to handle future misunderstanding by going through the same mental process.

- **Grants you forgiveness from your marriage mate and from God-** we all make mistakes, even daily at that. The fact that you are in a position to forgive your mate today does not mean tomorrow you will never find yourself in their situation, needing your mate's forgiveness. It is to be expected considering our own imperfect state. If you will like to be forgiven when you offend your spouse, why not extend forgiveness when they apologize for their own errors? Just as you want your mate to treat you, treat them the same way.

It has also been stated clearly in the Bible that if we want God to forgive us for our errors, we need to develop a forgiving spirit. A failure to forgive your spouse can result in God withholding his own forgiveness. So, will you really want to risk that over some form of misunderstanding?

Marriage is meant to be a long-lasting union. But sometimes some differences remain irreconcilable. One such difference is marital infidelity. When that happens, it is best not to think straight about divorce, even if that is a ground for divorce on its own. Think about the future, the long term good of your family, especially if you have children. Do not listen to family members and friends because they are only interested in nudging you to get even.

Some of these so-called advisers do not have a happy family so they might want to make a rash decision that will put you on the same level. You have the final decision of either to forgive your mate or to talk out. If you do either of them you have not sinned. So take your time and think about what is best for you in such circumstances.

REPENTANCE

To be a recipient of forgiveness, you must repent of your ill ways and turn around to the doing of good. This will tell your partner that it was just a mistake and never a deliberate attempt to hurt them. Repentance is a sincere feeling of regret over what has happened. Often times it comes with a remorseful feeling and a sincere apology. To be really repentant, however, is not easy as it requires real humility on the part of the erring one.

Forgiveness is not an easy thing to do either, but the offended partner needs to see proof that you are really repentant. In fact, it remains the key to the heart of your mate when feelings are hurt. As long as a man and woman live together as husbands and wives, they will always piss each other off once in a while. If mistakes are the plagues in a marriage, then repentance is the antidote. However, a humble admission that "I am wrong, please forgive me" is very hard for most marriage mates today because of pride and ego.

The Dangers of Pride

Pride is the opposite of humility. It is like that force suppressing the thoughts and desires of our hearts. Deep down you miss your partner's smile, the happy moments, you miss sharing your day with them and you only want that hug. But pride will be like the second voice in your head telling you things like "I am the head of this family and as such, I don't need to apologize" or "I'm sure he'll come back to me and apologize in no time". Pride will stop you from taking the necessary steps to mending the already strained relationship between you and your partner.

If allowed to reside in the mind, it will make a mountain of problems out of a molehill. The truth is that pride and ego have no place in the home of a happy couple. If you want your marriage to be successful,

Signs of a sincere Repentance

- **Apology-** This is the most obvious of all the signs that someone is truly repentant. The truth is that saying sorry is really a hard thing to do. This is because as imperfect humans, pride is inborn in us. But if your partner is willing to go down that line, then know that they really want to make things right. Don't make it hard for them as well, when they are willing to apologize, don't refuse their sincere apology if you want a happy home.

It is true that an apology must be sincere if it will work though. If you are the erring mate, make sure your apology is sincere because women especially are smart. They can detect when an apology is sincere or not.

- **Confession-** after apologizing for the wrong, the next thing you need to do is confess your errors, especially in cases of marital infidelity. This can also be a hard thing to do because it might mean recounting all the mistakes 'unedited' to your spouse. No matter what type of offense is involved, make sure you are honest about it from the start. If you are not plain and honest about it and your partner forgives you based on the edited version of events that you give, what do you think will happen when they find out the whole truth from another source sometimes later? This time you will not only have hurt them all over again, but you will also create doubt about stories in the future.

Confession can really be embarrassing, but who cares? It is you are your partner who knows almost everything about you. Your peace of mind, the happiness of your spouse, and the success of your marriage are far more important than any feeling of embarrassment that you may feel.

In cases where no serious wrongdoing is involved, you might simply own up to the mistake, admit that you are wrong. You can even mention what you did and how you plan to avoid such in the future. This will reassure your spouse that you are really committed to them.

- **Turning around-** What is the point of repentance if one does not plan to change their ways? It will all be a fruitless endeavor. So, if the cause of the problem is an improper friendship with another member of the opposite sex, and you have apologized to your spouse, what do you think you can do to really 'turn around'? Now is the time to put an end to that friendship once and for all. Remember that the approval you seek is coming from your spouse and not that friend posing a risk to your marriage.

If the issue involved is that of improper speech during an argument, can you always take a walk during a dispute with your wife? This way you will not fall into the trap of saying something that you will later regret. Up next is the value of Trust in a successful marriage.

KEY POINTS

- Before your spouse can think of forgiving you, it must be clear that you are sincerely repentance
- A sincere Repentance has three components: Confession, Apology, and a Turning around.
- When apologizing to your mate, make sure you are as honest as you can be. Chances are he might find out the truth later on and this can threaten the success of your marriage.

Chapter Six

RULE NO. 7- THE VALUE OF TRUST

If your marriage will thrive, be fulfilling, and successful, trust is very necessary. Trust is like profound confidence in your mate's person, ability, goals, and desires. When you trust your partner, you are absolutely sure of what they can or cannot do. This also will not be dependent on whether you are present or absent.

Trust is like cement or mortar that holds the building blocks of your marriage (Love and Respect) together. Apart from the fact that it holds a marriage together like glue, trust is also vital for your marriage to be a happy one. Without a measure of trust, it is most likely that the relationship won't ever graduate to the point of marriage in the first place. You will keep second-guessing their intentions. All you can do is hope for the best while you expect the worse out of fear.

It is like an assurance that this person will always be there for you in almost every situation you find ourselves. Trust, however, can only be expressed in actions and words. You need to do certain things for your spouse such that they will be sure where you really stand. No doubt most marriages today breaks down because of a lack of trust, which is evident in infidelity and other forms of marital betrayal.

Three reasons why you need trust in your marriage

- **You get the freedom to enjoy your marriage to the fullest**
  Most people never get to enjoy their marriage to the fullest, they never experience the heights of their emotions. This is because their marriage is plagued with a lack of trust. Love and intimacy are used as weapons to get back at the erring mate. When you also trust your spouse, there is absolutely nothing you won't be ready to share with them, even your deepest secrets. You can pour out your heart to them without any fear that what you tell them will be on the national news the very next day. But when there is enough trust in your marriage, when you are absolutely sure that your spouse has got your back, then you can really enjoy love, intimacy, and communication as it should be enjoyed in a marital setting.

- **You experience true freedom**
  A successful marriage should not be a prison where someone is restricted but an institution that allows marriage mates to express love and affection for each other anywhere they are. Without trust, that is never going to be possible. So ask yourself, 'how much love and affection is displayed in my marriage especially when we are in public'? If you feel that both are not in the appropriate measure, then that is a pointer that something needs to be done about the trust in your marriage. But the fact remains that trust only leads to true freedom between marriage mates.

- **You will both be prepared to weather the storm**

    If marriage is likened to a building, then the problems that face marriage today can also be likened to a storm. A storm can come from any direction the same way problems can come up even unannounced in a marriage. It could be health problems, childbearing issues, or even financial misunderstanding. Trust between a husband and his wife is the necessary ingredient that can enable a couple to cope well with any problems they both face. Trust will help them pull through together instead of thinking about their individual safety. As the years roll by, they will come to realize that the more they face those problems together, the stronger their bond will become.

It is clear that for a marriage to be successful, a couple must trust themselves really well. But just like a campfire, to keep the momentum of the burning, fuel is needed. And as time goes on, this same fuel needs to be replenished. The same is true of trust, it must be replenished from time to time as the couple grows older together.

This is because trust can be lost by the slightest of a wrong decision on the part of either the husband or wife. So, if you are a newly married couple, or you've been married for a long time, how can you 'keep up the momentum' of your trust? How can you replenish this trust too if you have ever broken the trust of your spouse?

Building and Rebuilding Trust in your Marriage

Every family member, either the husband or the wife surely wants the trust in their marriage to grow over time. But certain factors can break trust in a happy home. In a survey conducted among divorcees about what is most likely sure to break the trust in a marriage, these are the reasons mentioned:

1. Lies
2. Infidelity
3. Financial dishonesty
4. Insecurities
5. A sustained relationship with an ex
6. Emotional imbalance.

Looking at the factors above, it is clear that for a couple to remain happy by maintaining trust in their union, they need these two things:

- Communication
- Honesty

If these two are lacking, then you can never expect the trust in your relationship to be strong. And without a strong sense of trust, your marriage will never be a success. Let us take a look at the above-mentioned factors as it affects trust.

Communication

This subject has been treated in the preceding part of this book. You want your husband or wife to trust you, learn to share your feelings with them. You can't expect your wife to trust you with her secrets if you always withhold yours. If you want to hear about her day, why not take the lead and share how your day went. In today's busy world, it is all too easy to blame a lack of communication on a busy schedule.

But, if the success of your marriage is of prime importance to you, you will always create time to be with your spouse and enjoy a meaningful communication with them. The more you create time to be together, the more you communicate, and the more you communicate with them the stronger the bond that binds you will be. That right there is trust. So, if you ever feel that you have at one time broken the trust your spouse had in you, all hope is not lost.

Make it your aim to start spending time with them. Even if they find it hard pouring their hearts to you because of what you did, take the initiative and start by sharing your own day with them. Mention the challenges you faced that day. Constantly reassure them of your love. Don't expect them to change all of a sudden as this could take some time. But if you do not tire out, you will start seeing changes soon enough and you would have rebuilt the trust that has once collapsed.

Transparency

This is the number one reason why trust is lost in most marriages today. It always starts with one partner strongly feeling that the husband or wife is keeping something from them. So, they too start being cautious around them. Before long, both of them start acting cold and bitter towards each other, they start confiding in someone else (maybe a colleague at work or a friend), and if care is not taken, it could be the start of marital infidelity.

Always keep it in mind that to win the trust of your marriage mate, they need to know everything. Women especially love the details of issues, so if you as a man is being conservative about the truth, you are only contributing to the loss of trust in your home.

Learn to always tell the truth. Now the idea of truth should be the whole truth and not half-truth. Chances are if you are plain and honest in your conversations now, it will not just make your spouse happy and content, it will also make them believe you in the future. If you have at one time broken the trust your spouse had in you because of an unwise decision, why not return to telling the truth. It could be pivotal to rebuilding the lost trust in your marriage.

Project:

Determine today that you will start telling your marriage mate the whole truth. It could be embarrassing though to correct what you have told them before to be the truth. But it is worth the effort. You are creating a firm foundation for the trust in your marriage.

Think about all the relationships you have with members of the opposite sex that could be disturbing to your spouse. Take the bold step of ending such unions as this could jeopardize the trust your spouse has in you.

At the end of each day, take the lead in sharing with your spouse how the day went.

Chapter Seven

RULE NO. 8- AVOID RESENTMENT

Resentment is that ill-feeling that is caused by an unfair treatment or statement. It may look like a small it but it can ruin your marriage because it saps it of its happiness. The longer it stays, the harder it is to remove.

Resentment all stems from a deliberate desire to not forget the bad things being done or said by a marriage mate. The thoughts are fresh in the memory, and as such makes it hard to express any affection. Day after day, the joy is such a marriage will be gradually replaced by a resentful disposition. Even if your spouse tries to strike up a conversation, or try to do something that normally would have elicited a joyous reaction from you, you deliberately ignore it.

Resentment is like a marriage assassin that gradually creeps into the marriage without any of the couple planning for it. But once it's in already, will keep feeding on the ego of the marriage mates and will keep growing and gaining ground until it has siphoned all the happiness in the marriage.

It will eventually lead to a lack of communication, which can last for a long week, months, even years. Resentment can eat into almost every part of the relationship. The communication though is the first casualty, then it affects the respect, trust, intimacy, and also the capacity to forgive one's spouse when wronged in the union.

In this section of the book, we will look into how avoiding the temptation to resent your mate can contribute to the overall success of your marriage. This will take into consideration our imperfect nature as humans, with the nudge to resent others when wrong coming natural to us. First, we will look at the signs to look out for in order to know if you or your spouse are resentful. Next, we will examine what you can do to avoid resentment in your marriage.

Resentment Signals

No one likes to be resented. It harms both parties no matter how much they lie to themselves about it. Often times it leads to a subtle kind of hatred between the couple. So, how can you know you are been resented? How can you determine if you are being resentful as well?

- Silent treatment- when you start noticing that they really reduce conversations with you, especially if they are the type that talks naturally. They may stop sharing the good moments of their day with you, stop responding to funny jibes, and totally stop smiling back at you when they are supposed to. When you see all this signal, know that your partner resents you for a reason.

- Unusual Aggression- Sometimes, a spouse may get angry at the slightest provocation due to an underlying cause of resentment. If you find out that your spouse is irked up even at little things when you know they shouldn't be, be aware that your partner may be reacting to something.

- Intentional abandonment of responsibility- you are used to the chores your wife will never abandon but all of a sudden, you notice that they always leave it to chance and in other cases, they stop doing them totally. Maybe your husband is always happy to give you some money for some personal endeavors but all of a sudden he stops giving you the money all of a sudden even though he has the money. If you start noticing these symptoms, know that your marriage might be under an attack from resentment.

- Sexual Starvation- for one thing, everyone enjoys sex except a few. Maybe you notice your spouse who is always excited by the thought of making love to you but stops the craving all too suddenly. That is another signal that your marriage is under attack.

These are not the only signals but are the common ones. Some partners might start screaming and arguing unnecessarily with you, others might stop updating you about their movements, while others may stop confiding in you altogether. Whichever way your partner reacts, be observant of these signals as they can ruin a marriage if not attended to promptly.

Now, if you do not want resentment to ruin your happy marriage, understand that sometimes your partner will react to some things due to discontent. We are imperfect and as such we will definitely offend each other.

The results of resentment are very dangerous. It can create a void or distance between you and your spouse. You and your partner won't be able to readily arrive at a reasonable compromise when issues occur. It is like the emotional bridge between you two is broken and it can make the resentment to be even deeper.

When there is a resentful atmosphere at home, trust is easily broken. Take for example when one couple can no longer confide in the other because of a feeling of hurt that is perceived but never trashed out properly in a peaceful dialogue. They will be forced to start confiding in another member of the opposite sex. The more this situation goes on, the closer they both are to marital infidelity. How sad that will be if they both allow that to happen, all in the name of resentment.

If marital infidelity is allowed to creep in, that can end the marriage as they both won't trust each other again.

To achieve the goal of a happy marriage, resentment should not be allowed to stay, for too long at that. How can you prevent, or even take necessary steps in order to eliminate this threat?

How to prevent a prolonged resentment

One thing you should understand is that as humans, we will at one point or the other resent others or be resented. But as a couple even though you both experience this once in a while, you must both be careful not to prolong the resentment more than necessary. Here are some steps to take in other not to be trapped in the cage of prolonged resentment.

Talk it out- a major cause of a prolonged resentment is assumption without confirmation. A spouse might suspect something but may never discuss it with their partner. The result of that is a reaction that may be baseless as the perceived cause was never properly addressed. Immediately you perceive something that is not right with you, speak to your marriage mate about it immediately. Be prepared not to allow resentment to raise its ugly head in your home.

If the resentment is as a result of an argument at home, take the first step by calling your husband or wife to talk it out. Make sure proving your innocence and apportioning blame is not the purpose of the discussion, but the peace of your home.

Learn to forgive- when hurt feelings are left unattended to, grudges linger, and then reactions follow. Here is what you can do to curb that: understand that your spouse is imperfect. Imperfect people make mistakes and when you understand that, you will not react every time you make mistakes. The more you forgive the more you are ridding your marriage of a prolonged resentment.

Commendation- when you learn to appreciate others, especially your spouse in simple ways, you are laying a foundation of happiness in your marriage. So, always look out for areas that need commendation in your marriage mate. Did they achieve something at work? Did they do something right at home? Learn to appreciate them. Even if they are resentful to you, chances are the more you appreciate them the softer their mind will become.

Refrain from Stalking your partner-There is something that happens when you secretly stalk your marriage mate: you will always find a reason to resent them. If you suspect that your spouse is cheating on you, possibly because of a perceived emotional distance between that on its own is a cause for resentment. But how will it look like if you pick up their mobile devices and start going through their private messages? Most likely you will see some things that greatly affect your relationship negatively. Because the stalking was done without their knowledge, you will start reacting negatively toward them. That will only add to the resentment already on the ground. So the antidote is simple: make a conscious effort never to stalk your marriage mate. It really helps in keeping a prolonged resentment at bay.

The more your effort in avoiding resentment, the more you are training yourself and building your marriage to be successful. No marriage is perfect, but you can find joy in spite of the imperfection evident in your marriage.

Key Points

- Resentment is normal in any healthy relationship, but a prolonged resentment is very dangerous.
- Resentment can ruin your marriage because it forms a basis for many other vices in most marriages.
- Most marital infidelity is a result of a prolonged resentment.

Chapter Eight

RULE NO. 9- PROPER VIEW OF SEXUAL INTIMACY

To some people, when they are asked what makes a marriage strong, they often mention sexual intimacy. They are not wrong as this really can have a bearing on the depth of a relationship, even marriage. A couple that has more sex are closer to each other than a couple that rarely has sex. However, for sexual intimacy to really do its work, it must be viewed properly as a means to an end, and not the end itself. This is because a happy marriage takes a lot more than just making love to each other.

The marriage arrangement is the only legal, biblical and moral way to enjoy sex. That translates to mean that when couples keep sex within the marital arrangement, they don't feel guilty after sex, they are happier after sex, and they learn to trust each other more. That is what differentiates it from premarital sex as well as takes affairs. Both of these comes with the worries and anxieties of guilt. But in the marital arrangement, you can enjoy sex the way it is meant to be enjoyed.

It is one way to draw closer to each other in a very special way. But, with every privilege comes the responsibility of not misusing it. It is true that you can use fire in a controlled setting to boil some things and make them tastier, but something disastrous can happen if the same fire is not controlled. So, if sex is not viewed properly, it can sap a marriage mate of his or her joy in the marriage.

Principle of mutual Agreement

If you both are to view sex properly, it is imperative for both of you to see sex as something that must be mutually agreed upon for it to serve its purpose. In a healthy relationship, sex should not be demanded nor must it be forced. That is what makes rape very painful because it is done against someone's will. So, recognize that your husband or wife deserves some form of respect and dignity. Learn to respect their decisions sometimes especially as it relates to sexual intimacy between you two.

It is also good for you to understand that there are sometimes that your partner might not be in the mood. For example, there are some days in a month that a woman is menstruating. Often times, women are a little bit edgy during these periods of the month. From a recent survey, most married women agreed that sexual intimacy during these times is not something they are less interested in.

Men on the other hand also find it hard getting intimate when they are having bad days or when they are frustrated. Whichever the case is, understanding that your mate might not be feeling like you are is the first step to enjoying sexual intimacy in your marriage.

Consider what will happen if you were to force sex on your husband or wife. They may give in, but will they really enjoy it? Hardly! They may start seeing you as selfish, they may be scared of you, or even lose respect for you. But when you both consider each other's emotional makeup and physical circumstances, you will be cultivating a proper view of sex, which in turn will contribute immensely to the success of your marriage. Remember, for you to really enjoy your sex life, it must always be mutual and never forced.

Tips for Improving Your Sex Lives

Be Romantic

When some people think about romance, what their mind goes straight to s what happens in the bedroom. But that word is broader than just that. It is good to always prepare the ground before stepping on it so to speak. Making your spouse feel good is as important as sexual intimacy itself. So, plan for some dinner dates where you will get to talk and get connected really well. If you are at work, it will be also nice if you can send a text message to your mate telling them how much you love them and how eager you will like to get home just so you can be with them. It could even be called just to say you miss them. Little things like these can go a long way to get you emotionally on par with your partner.

Make do with what you have

Sometimes, you may not have the luxury of the kind of date locations or the fancy vacations you used to have. All you may now have is just a few minutes together after a stressful day at work. You may not be living alone as you might have kids. In whatever situation you find yourself, you can still enjoy a great time together intimately. If all you have together after each day is about 2 hours, be determined to make it count with your partner. Even if you are not making love to each other that night, try to sleep in each other's arms at least. If you already have kids, make sure their bedroom is separated from the room you share with an hour partner. Lock the doors so that they don't spoil the mood at some point. Other people may find it helpful to put off all gadgets so as to keep the 'alone time' really special.

Learn the art of a 'Quickie

In the past, you may have been very reluctant to try out a quickie because it just doesn't suit you, well it may be one thing you will learn to try out. Because of the busy schedules of people today, a quickie might just be what they need in order to keep their sex life alive. Another crucial time in a marriage when a quickie can come very handy is when you become a parent. A great part of your energy will be spent on the new member of the family. So, a quickie may really be the best thing you both can hang on to in order to keep the fire of intimacy burning. One thing you can also do is fantasize as much as possible. Think about the beautiful times you have had in times past, and let those cherished memories keep you as fresh as ever.

Don't be so boring

They say if you keep doing the same things over and over again, you will get bored sooner or later. The same is true of your sex life as a couple. So, if you want to avoid this eventuality, make sure you try out new things. Explore your entire intimate lifestyle and see how you can improve on it. If your mate suggests a new style to your sex life, don't be reluctant to try it out as it could be the thing that will make them keep enjoying intimacy within your marriage. A word of caution though is that sexual relations are sweeter if it is done the right way. So, even though you want to be adventurous, make sure it doesn't endanger your marriage mate. If it does, it will take away the enjoyment in it.

Another thing you can do to spice things up is to change your location once in a while. We are not suggesting that you relocate every two or three years. You can take some time off for a vacation and you two stay in a hotel for a couple of days. You will be amazed at how this will improve your sex life.

Communicate

If couples want to keep enjoying their sex life, it is vital for them to always communicate. There is no other way to let your partner know what you want other than talking about it. If there is a particular thing that you would want to be done differently, talk about it. Don't be shy about it; you are talking to the most important person to you. But be careful not to talk about how much you want your partner to improve at something while you both are making love. Such a discussion can wait until when you are doing something else.

Chapter Nine

RULE NO. 10 – HONESTY

In this world we live in, honesty is something that has become all but lost. A man and his wife should really have nothing to hide from each other, they should be plain with themselves as this will make them trust each other.

Naturally, humans are very honest and innocent, but many get affected by the common trend the 'you do not need to be plain honest with your spouse'. But where exactly has this trend led many couples today? Dishonesty today is one of the leading causes of marital failure today. Some people hide virtually everything from their spouses, from text messages to calls, to income. Some years ago, there was this story circulating in one part of Africa about a man who packed his bags and left home because he found out that the house where they have been paying rent for the past 10 years is actually owned by the wife.

One excuse people give for being dishonest is the fact that they don't want to hurt the feelings of their marriage mate. But is lying really going to keep them safe? Chances are when the truth finally gets out, they will feel hurt more than they might have been if they have been told the truth. So, being dishonest in this scenario only does more harm than good.

Psychologists have also found out that the benefits of being honest with your marriage mate far outweigh the risks. Let us briefly examine the dangers posed by lies in marriage.

How the Dangers of Dishonesty

Lies always starts from the little ones, often told to save one from disgrace or shame. These little lies may not be done to harm your spouse or to deceive them in any major ways. But as these little lies continue, it gets to a point where telling lies to save face becomes easier. Sooner or later bigger lies will creep in and in no time, you become a perpetual liar.

Lying is a chain reaction; if you tell one lie, you will most likely tell another lie to cover it up. You will then fall into the trap of keeping an accurate record of all the lies you've told just in case you are asked again. But think for a moment again to all the vows you took not to hurt that special person to you. Is lying really the best way to keep those vows? That is highly disrespectful to your spouse.

If your spouse eventually finds out that you have been telling a series of lies, they will start doubting all the things you have ever told them. It will eventually lead to a situation where all the trust they had in you will have been all but lost. Will you really want that to happen all just to save your face a couple of times?

If you are to enjoy a very happy marriage, there must be a mutual form of respect. Dishonesty is as bad a vice in a marriage that it can make you lose the respect of your spouse. But imagine how that respect will build up over time if things were as transparent between you two.

Always keep it in mind that to win the trust of your marriage mate, they need to know everything. Women especially love the details of issues, so if you as a man is being conservative about the truth, you are only contributing to the loss of trust in your home.

Learn to always tell the truth. Now, the idea of truth should be the whole truth and not half-truth. Chances are if you are plain and honest in your conversations now, it will not just make your spouse happy and content, it will also make them believe you in the future. If you have at one time broken the trust your spouse had in you because of an unwise decision, why not return to telling the truth. It could be pivotal to rebuilding the lost trust in your marriage

In the marital arrangement, honesty is manifested not only in what is said but also in what is done. A husband or wife who is honest with his or her partner will not be claiming to love their mate while doing things that are contrary to what they say. Such things will include flirting with another member of the opposite sex either at work or elsewhere. They will not be secretly viewing pornography, which could hurt their mate if they find out. They will also try hard to stay true to the vows they made by not going online for some form of emotional attachment.

Dangers of Dishonesty

Frequent arguments- The more dishonest you are, the more you are likely to play down their enormity when confronted with them. This will not go down well with your partner as you both are bound to have arguments upon arguments every single time this happens. And when arguments are too frequent, it might get to the point where you and your mate are no longer open to any agreement.

Trust issues- Trust is a total reliance on someone, an expectation of fairness, and full confidence in their ability to always have your back. When you are dishonest, or worse still, on a number of occasions, it takes all that away. You are no longer that person they always want to fall back on. They start getting suspicious of all your utterances. The disappointing eventuality to trust issues is that even when you are being truthful, you will still be doubted.

Emotional distance- after a series of dishonest sayings and acts, you may find out that your mate no longer feels comfortable sharing their innermost thoughts with you. As you are no longer their confidant, they will find someone else with whom they are comfortable sharing thoughts. If that person happens to be a member of the opposite sex, they may soon be drawing closer to that person emotionally, while going further apart from you.

Unhappy Marriage- Imagine a marriage where all the three points mentioned above are a common thing. If a home is permeated by arguments every single day, they have trust issues, and there is a palpable discord between the couple, then the marriage becomes an unhappy one. They will just be enduring the union instead of enjoying it. This is a long-term effect of dishonesty in a marriage.

Conquering Dishonesty

It may look like an unpopular opinion but it is something that is worth the effort. No one will build your home for you as you are the architect of your marriage's success or failure. Friends will tell you that you are being soft or not man enough, but they are secretly doing what it takes to build their own home too without telling you. So, be determined today to start being transparent with your spouse.

If you are honest in your dealings, your husband or mate will see and feel it. It will be evident in how your marriage mate relates to you. It will prompt them to be plain with you too. If they notice that you are been honest with your income they too will share everything needed with you as per their own earnings too.

If you want a happy and successful marriage, you need to keep your spouse happy. Being honest with them is one way of keeping them happy. Even though people are not encouraging this beautiful habit, learn it, treasure it, and keep your marriage as happy as it should be. The next recipe we will discuss is patience and how it can help you enjoy your marriage.

RULE NO. 11- PATIENCE

Patience they say is a virtue. As a husband or a wife, you need to cultivate this beautiful quality if you will enjoy living with your spouse. Patience is a quality you need either you are a husband or a wife as you will both be tested overtime in your marriage.

When many hear the word patience, what comes to their mind is waiting for a very long time. But patience is broader than that. It is the ability to endure an unpleasant situation without giving up. It can also mean bearing up without getting easily provoked. As earlier mentioned, there will be times when your partner will test your temper. Consider some harmful effects of impatience in a marriage.

Dangers

Loss of respect- no one wants to live with a partner that easily flares up at every slight provocation. It is a sign of stupidity to always do that and if care is not taken, it can cause serious issues and over time can make your spouse lose respect for you.

Fights- People who are impatience are prone to arguments and quarrels with their spouses. With more quarrels comes more fights and that can never be a passport to a happy marriage. It will only impact negatively on the marriages.

Debt- Impatient people are too frustrated with having to wait for tasks o be executed. Hence all they want is to see it done as fast as possible, even though they can't afford it. They can go into debt just to achieve their aim. Well, this is not a good thing for the family as it would affect their finances negatively in the long run.

Alcohol abuse- Because waiting isn't their thing, they want to forget about the frustration at all costs. This they do most times with alcohol and drugs. All this can become distasteful to the spouse and children if they have.

Emotional distance- the long-term impact of impatience on the part of either the husband or wife is that leads to an emotional distance between them. Instead of drawing closer to each other, the opposite will be the case.

Cultivating Patience

Don't expect perfection- You are imperfect, and so is your spouse. Don't expect them to be perfect with what they do. There will be times that they will make mistakes, just as you too will make some mistakes. So give allowances for the mistakes and you will find yourself happy and your marriage better.

Be self-controlled- Self-control is the ability to remain calm in the face of provocation. Couples will argue once in a while and while this is bound to happen, something must be done to prevent each situation from escalating into a very ugly situation.

Practice it daily- If you try it on a daily basis, you will eventually become a patient person to your spouse as well as kids. So, try to keep calm when your family members make mistakes. Be kind to them as much as you can. It takes time so practice it daily.

Let Love lead- Remember that love is patient; it is kind and does not get easily provoked. If you allow the love you have for your partner to prevail, you will not be too mad at them when they make a mistake. As you cultivate kindness in words and actions, your husband or wife will come to appreciate you more and find comfort in your company.

Better mental health- Your peace of mind is pretty much important too, so calm down and don't drive yourself too crazy when things don't go your way. If you get too involved in very little arguments that could be avoided, you will eventually see that it will start affecting how you reason and think. A more calm approach will make things easier for you and for your spouse. You will keep yourself fresh for other productive activities, which could improve your marriage.

It helps your forgiveness- Patience is the quality that motivates a forgiving spirit. So, the more patient you are, the more forgiving you will become. And what is more? A successful marriage is the union of two good forgivers.

If you want your marriage to be successful, more comfort in your home, more laughs, it is a worthwhile endeavor trying to cultivate patience. Chances are the more patient you are with your spouse, the better prepared they too will be in reciprocating such quality. And as you both lay a good foundation for this quality; you are only preparing your children too for this great challenge.

Chapter Ten

RULE NO. 12- SPEND TIME WITH EACH OTHER

Reasons you should think more about spending time together

There are a number of reasons why you should create time for being with your marriage mate. Let us consider a few.

A healthy relationship- if your marriage is to be successful, you need to regularly find time to be with your spouse. The more you stay together the better you know them. You will get to know your partner so well that without them telling you something, you already know what they want.

Better chance of solving issues amicably- because when you spend time with someone, you will piss each other off more and makeup faster. So as greater causes for quarrel come up, it becomes easier to solve such problems. So, if you want to have a successful relationship with your marriage mate, you should spend more time with your spouse for this reason.

A happier marriage- it is true that when we love someone, we will spend more time with them. As you spend more time with your spouse whom you love more, you become happier, and this happiness will radiate into your marriage.

You will last long as a couple- one of the causes of divorce is a lack of quality time together. So as you spend more time with your spouse, you will only allay any fear of divorce that could come in the future.

You spice things up- when you decide to spend time with your partner, it is most of the time done in a very special place. You can visit places like the zoo, or an aquarium or even travel to another monumental location. All these can breathe life into a relationship and even in your long-term union.

How to make time for your spouse

The burning question about spending time together as a couple is all about TIME. We are all so busy; family heads are busy trying to provide for their wives and kids, a wife at home might be busy with their daily multitasking- combining a secular career with household chores. Even if you both have earmarked some time to spend together, what about unforeseen events at work? Where will the kids stay?

Carefully consider the following points as it will help you both care for all these questions while you are both determined to make your marriage a success by spending time with your husband or wife.

Plan way ahead of time- If you both will spend time together; decide well in advance in the year when you both will be willing to take a vacation during the year. Once you both have identified a particular time of the year that you will both be free, start making plans to be free. If you leave it late before making such plans, you may never find the time as priorities could change either at work or within the family.

Prepare where to keep your children- If you don't have kids yet, this may not be something you need to do. But assuming you have kids already, you should start talking to family and friends that you are confident your children will be comfortable staying around about the possibility of housing your children for a couple of days you will not be around.

Prepare to have some fun- all work and no play they say make 'jack' a dull boy. Why not think of going somewhere that might give you both an opportunity to have fun? Ask you mate what activities they consider fun. Pick one or two activities that you are sure you both will enjoy like going to the cinema, attending a music concert, watching a live match in a stadium or just enjoying the sight of beautiful places.

Watch out whom you let keep your kids- while you are away, you are still responsible for the safety of your children if you have any. Make sure you are careful when choosing who you'll let take care of your kids while you are gone. This modern era has seen child sexual abusers become many. Most times, these abusers are people both the parents and kids' trust. So if a particular friend or family is known for any questionable behavior in the past, don't let your children stay with them.

Let others help you- if you own a business and you are scared of how it will fare when you are away, you may never find that time to spend with your marriage mate. So, if you have employees, trust them to take good care of your business while you are away. Give them clear instructions on what you want them to help you with.

Without traveling, you can still decide to spend some time together daily after work. Here's what you can do: make sure you come home straight after work. This will afford you both a couple of hours more days than usual.

If you are the shy type, clueless as to what to do when you are alone with your spouse, well we will give you a few ideas. While everything isn't about sexual intimacy, there are things you can do that will draw you guys closer to each other. Trust me; the biggest challenge is to find that time that you will be spending together. When you both have gotten a time frame together, you only need to consider these few options.

Enjoy a relaxing moment

You both could treat yourself to time at the spa. You will be surprised how much you both will enjoy the treatment. You could also try some other relaxation and massaging techniques; that helps you discover what you enjoy the most. If you or your spouse knows how to give a very good massage, you can do it while in your hotel room.

A gentle massage is a great way to relax and spend quality time together, and we'd highly recommend it.

Eat out

One thing you can do is to plan a special eating out package for yourselves on special days. You can pick every Sunday or Monday for that. Visit a special restaurant and free yourselves from cooking at home for those special days. The food and drinks you both will enjoy will be somewhat different from what you are used to. It will also afford you both an opportunity to enjoy meaningful conversations. No doubt this will draw you closer to each other.

Go to the Cinema

Some couples have forgotten about how to see a movie together because after they got married they thought these activities are no longer necessary again. But planning this, on very special occasion of maybe your anniversary will no doubt remain indelibly etched in the mind of your spouse. Ask your partner what movie they will like to see, and threat yourselves to a nice day out in the cinema. Accompany this with some soda and popcorn. The laughs you will have will prove to be memorable.

Take a walk once in a while

There are times that we are just too stressed out and we might decide to take a walk by seeing nature at its best. It could be the zoo or an aquarium, or simply walking down a street and enjoying the fresh air coming directly from nature. Well, don't go alone the next time; make sure you go with your spouse and see how much fun you both will have.

Plan Romantic Nights

This is easier to do when you are without kids. You can make special dishes and light fancy candle on your dining table. Another thing you can do on occasions is taking your bath together. It might seem like an awkward idea but you will love it. Stay for a while in the bathtub and discuss while you both maintain that intimate disposition. If you already have kids, you can leave them in care of a babysitter or you can have a relative pick them up for the weekend. And if your children are grown, you can decide to have these romantic nights in a hotel.

Include it in your plans

Early in the year, when putting stuffs in your calendar and the likes, make sure you include the times you want to spend entirely with your spouse in the yearly schedule. It could be a location that you plan to visit, like the romantic city of Paris and the ancient city of Rome. These avenues with provide you both with some 'alone' time. You can even take such vacation more than once in a year. The first can be around March or April while the other could be later in the year like November or December.

It is really worth your while because spending time with your spouse will only make things better in your marriage and contributes to your marriage. So never underestimate what spending time with your mate can do to a dying relationship. It will breathe life into it and make it healthy again.

From today on, make a conscious effort to include the time you will spend with your marriage mate in your plans, and stick to it. Invest your time and effort in it and watch your marriage blossom like and lilies.

RULE NO. 13- COOPERATION/TEAMWORK

Imagine that you are doing teamwork alone, you will only toil for long hours and achieve very little. The sad truth is that many couples don't see marriage as teamwork; hence they try to push through activities alone and only find out that they are frustrated at the end of the day.

Everything in a marriage, from simple decision making to childrearing everything must be done together. When those things are done together, the burden will seem heavy and the result will always be an unhappy marriage.

A successful marriage is a two-person teamwork, one that is to be filled by you and your marriage mate. A recent survey has found out those marriages in which the parties involved see themselves as teammates are more likely to exhibit greater wisdom and more stability.

How will marriage without the teamwork orientation fare? Think of how a football team that focuses on individual brilliance will fare against another football team that prizes teamwork over individuality. The difference will definitely be a monumental whooping of a lifetime by the team that plays together over the team that focuses on individual efforts.

What is the lesson? Learn to always cooperate with your partner in a marriage. You can't do everything alone as this will only complicate matters in your union. Your marriage will be devoid of all the ingredients it should have like fun, support system, goals, leadership, chemistry, and cooperation.

If you decide to do everything alone, even you will not be happy with the result.

Teamwork is one of the most important aspects of maintaining a strong marriage.

What does that look like in a stable, loving marriage?

Teamwork is when two people work together for the good and betterment of their life. In a marriage, teamwork requires several components to be successful.

Communication between two people is the first step. When communicating our needs, desires, and wishes we open the door to seeing something we both want to become a reality. The common phrase, "Two heads are better than one," works well here, especially when it comes to teamwork. Two people may be able to solve the problem that an individual cannot. Without consistent communication, your relationship will become unsatisfying and distant.

In every marriage, a solid commitment must be present or the lifelong love you professed to one another becomes threatened, and sooner or later the marriage will fall apart.

How often do you fail to compromise in your marriage? Part of being an effective team player is to see the big picture. This requires a willingness to be open to your spouse's ideas, seeing their vision as being possible, and whether you agree with their vision or not, being willing to support them wholeheartedly.

It doesn't do your marriage any good to compete with each other or let one person do all the work. Through teamwork, you use both the partner's talents and abilities to get the job done.

Even though you may have your different careers and you may both be successful, you can choose to help each other out instead of trying to outshine one another.

Two people in a healthy marriage set goals to achieve together. They talk with each other about the dreams they want to reach as a couple and they share their own personal dreams that will help them continue to strengthen their own purpose in life.

Working together as a team grows the love between you and strengthens the bond you want to cherish.

You can speak with your spouse and itemize areas you both can really work together more. It could be in the area of correcting your kids, how you want to have each other's back more than you currently do. What if you are already cooperating enough, try to do it more as there is always room for improvement. Discuss what good it will do you and your marriage. View yourselves as a team and what teammate do is work together. If it will help, mention specific areas you can do better. The more you work together; your children will learn the importance of teamwork from you and your partner.

If you feel that presently you and your spouse are really worlds apart in this aspect, what can you do? Are you feeling like you and your spouse currently exists at complete polar ends? Do you no longer communicate effectively and have the commitment you once felt slipped away?

It can be scary to experience these feelings in your relationship. When you committed yourself to one another you promised to be there for each other. You may be asking yourself, "So, what happened?"

You forgot to remember that there are two people involved in a marriage and together you are a force to be reckoned with, but apart there is no stable foundation. Being together should mean you have each other's back. The strength you have together should bring two people closer.

A marriage requires maintenance and being there through the good, bad and ugly times of life. Isn't that what we promised each other on the day we were married?

Sometimes, we just need to give each other that needed nudge or reminder that we are there for each other.

You need teamwork to maintain a strong marriage. In fact, it is one of the most important things in your marriage toolbox. Teamwork makes you both work together and try to create good and better life for yourselves.

So don't compete with one another, it's no good. Don't also feel like one person has to do all the work. The best team is one that makes use of the strengths and abilities of all on the team to get the work done, not one that exploits the abilities of others while saving theirs. So always set goals together and draw plans on how you will reach them. Be open about where you want to be together and share where you'd personally wish to be. The more you work together, the stronger the bonds that hold you together.

KEY POINTS

- Marriage is not a competition between you and your spouse. The more you cooperate with each other, the more successful your marriage will become.
- No matter how busy you may be, find time to always be with your partner.

Chapter Eleven

RULE NO. 14- CONTROL YOUR ANGER

Fear, worries, sadness, loss, disappointment, discouragement are types of emotions found underneath the anger. Anger is a strong emotional feeling that can kill or trigger potentially deadly rhythms in certain vulnerable people. Every day, both parties in marriage face or experience situations that bring them close to feelings of anger. When not properly checked, the marital knots could be loosened. Anger management is all about recognizing that you are getting angry. It also is when you take conscious action to calm down and deal with the issue.

Common causes of anger

Parental Example
If children will learn vital qualities and characters while growing up, they will learn almost 80 percent from their parents. Since children spend most of their time with their parents at home, they most likely will have more influence on their personality. No wonder kids learn to react to situations the same way they see their parents react to similar situation. They copy the way they talk, the way they make certain gestures and the way they express anger.

Some children are raised in a very hostile home with tempers flaring in the most awkward way over very frivolous reasons. When these children grow up, they too will model their reactions over trivial matters after the way they were used to- the situation back at home. When they too are faced with daily challenges when they grow up, their reactions are all too easy to predict. Children are like cushions that can suck the waters around where they are placed. Similarly, their brain is so sharp that it can pick up any behavior that they are exposed to during these formative years.

Personal Problems

When things don't go as planned, the only thing we do most times is to be anxious. For example, in most countries around the world, the level of unemployment is plummeting at a geometric rate. A recent report states that there are some 250 million people around the world are jobless. In some parts of Africa, university graduates flood the street because of unemployment. Family crises is the cause of some people's anxieties, while for others, the death of a loved one can cause these feelings. When people are anxious, they tend to react in anger to challenging situations that tend to stress them the more.

Illness is another personal problem many people are battling with. They are so downcast by their health condition that they tend to be angry when things are not done in a way that favors them. So if your partner is facing a major challenge in their life, know that this will increase their chances of getting angry at trivial situations.

Injustice

In one part of the world after another, injustices are common. Governments are getting more and more corrupt, citizens are deprives the basic amenities needed to enjoy life, health bills are killing faster than the disease, and without the needed 'connections' you can't afford food. Tribalism, racism, and other forms of favoritism is also another cause for an angry response from people. When one comes from a minority race or tribe that have been victimized over a long period of time, they will be so used to reacting very angrily to certain situations that ordinarily should not evoke an angry response.

Social Media and Television

Some people are only angry because of what they expose themselves to in the form of entertainment. Social media these days make it look harmless if you purchase a gun and use it. Music videos are filled with violence all in the name of entertainment and people see this as normal. The result is an angry atmosphere among viewers. They are more brutal in their approaches and they tend to show less mercy and compassion in how they relate with people. They come to see anger as a way of easing themselves of unpleasant situations. All these can contribute to aggression in a marriage mate's disposition, which could be transferred to the marriage.

Why a lack of anger management is harmful to your marriage

Whatever extent you fuel the flames of love in your marital life, determines how much joy and satisfaction you derive from it. Constantly getting mad at each other at every little spark can go a long way to detract from your desire to fuel the flames of love. Just as anger can shorten your lifespan, it can shorten the lifespan of your marriage. A University of Michigan study was done over a 17 year period found that couples that hold in their anger have a shorter lifespan than those who really say they are mad.

Further, a major disadvantage of becoming angry is that fiery emotions and adrenaline in one's system often exclude rational thoughts. Such a situation is dangerous. You will almost regret things said or done in anger. The time that should have been devoted to discussing the family's progress would be channeled to talks of apology about what had been wrongly expressed in anger.

Marriage is a perfect avenue to learn how to manage one's anger because in marriage you will experience almost all negative emotions. Hurts, frustration and anxiety often are common to marriage mates. But there are better ways to deal with these issues instead to giving a free rein to anger. When your partner does something you don't like, it is common to be advised by friends and colleagues to get back at him. They will tell you that you have a right to "pay him back in his own coin" or "get your pound of flesh back". While these ideas could sound appealing, they can really make things turn from bad to worse.

Holding on to anger will only hurt you more than you should. Anger will result into an aggressive attitude which is evident in the yelling and screaming and 'calling each other names' that is common among some marriage couples today. This will not make you both happy, and it can't make your marriage successful. If these things cannot help your marriage when problems occur, what can really help you? Consider the following helpful tips.

Be Patient with your spouse

If a marriage will really live up to its good name, hurling abuses and insults has no place in it. What these vices do is that it makes the home inhabitable for you and your partner. Most times, these stuffs happen because of the pride or ego of marriage mates. The truth is, when you are wronged, take a moment to breathe in and out, and then think about what you want to say. If you are aware that your anger might cause you to say things you don't want to say, you can take a walk. Before you return, things will have calmed down and you will be in a better position to control your tongue and thoughts.

Be Forgiving

Understand that just as your mate errs against you, you too can err against them. You are both imperfect, meaning they will make mistakes. So when they make these little mistakes, even though you can be angry, don't hold on to such anger for too long.

Communicate honestly

If you really love your spouse, it is vital that you express yourself in a calm and loving manner even if you are angry. Don't allow anger block that part of your brain that reminds you that you are talking to your husband or wife. If that part is not blocked out, you will tell them whatever it is you want with love and not in anger. It is true that you might feel the hurt but remember that your goal is a successful marriage. No matter how much you feel the hurt, never forget this fact

RULE NO. 15- BE FLEXIBLE WITH FINANCES

One of the leading causes of divorce presently is money or financial matters. The difference in opinion and ideas often lead to irreconcilable strain and eventual separation. It has been observed that most couples might have had a very different view of money and what it can buy before marriage. When these ones get married, it will be hard merging these varying views. When money matters come up, these differing opinions can cause very serious issues that will take away the peace in the marriage.

It is true that money can never buy love, but money matters and disagreement can tear a marriage apart. It can cause fights and quarrel as a long-held belief about money is not easy to change. Money can have a great deal of bearing on life goals. And if a couple's life goals do not tally along well, they might never be really happy as couple.

For some people, they are not cool with operating a joint bank account while another one might insist on a joint account. Some people are keen on buying material things like phones and fast cars. Others are interested in owning properties like houses and lands. All these different opinions can cause a measure of friction in the marriage.

So, if you want a happy and successful marriage, what can you do? How can you handle these differences? You can cater to these things by calling your marriage mate and having a dialogue with them about how to reach a reasonable compromise. Some other things that you need to also do are talk about your goals and find a way of aligning them. If you can have this kind of conversation with your spouse, you have surmounted the first hurdle in overcoming financial issues between you two.

A Realistic Conversation

When it comes to such dialogues, the earlier the better. Most couples leave this kind of talk until the time they need to make such decisions. It is true that talking about finances can be quite uncomfortable, but discussing it well in advance is really worth it. If one person wants to be frugal and the other wants to live lavish, it is the time to understand each other. When discussing such changes, be mindful of the different upbringing, which might play a role in how your spouse thinks about money and what money can buy. Regardless of what their thought process might be like, call your spouse and them; you will like to have a conversation about your future. Even if your spouse wants a joint or a separate account, they will definitely be interested in discussing what the future holds for you both.

Analyze what your earnings are, how often you will like to go on vacations, how much you'd like to spend on groceries, food, clothing, and so on. You can also talk about how much you will like to spend on arranging the home, the gadgets you will use, and how much you plan to spend on your in-laws. If you have this kind of discussion well in advance, it won't be a real problem when you are to make such decisions.

While talking about those things, expect that sometimes what you want or how much you suggest might be different from what your spouse wants. Remember that your goal is to talk about it amicably and maintain happiness in your marriage. So, when their opinion is different and you know yours is better, don't impose your view on them. Rather calmly discuss why you think your idea is better. Be ready to yield in some ways as you can't always have your way. This will make them happy as well.

Don't be discouraged that your first meeting to talk it out may not be what you expected- all smooth. Even if you disagree, don't give up, find another time and discuss all pressing financial issue.

Be Frank with Yourselves
Emotions might flare up sometimes, and that's to be expected. But if allowed to turn into a prolonged quarrel, the discussion might not lead to a reasonable compromise. So when discussing such issues with your spouse, refrain from using languages that are tainted with emotional hurt or frustration. Don't use accusations and degrading terms to humiliate your spouse's view of finances. And don't be too quick to blame your marriage mate for a change in your family's financial fortune. Even when it is obvious that they made a serious error in judgment in the past, don't use it as a weapon during your arguments. Don't be too critical but be frank. Say things the exact way they are without having to shame them or an action they took.

Remember the aim of the discussion is to find a working formula so be clear with your intentions. Once you both arrive at a solution, note it and you can even write them down. So again, this discussion isn't one to be used to criticize your partner, not their past decision. It is also expected that your spouse will be frank with you too. So, don't feel upstaged when your spouse mentions something about your financial habits that need to be corrected.

Come up with a plan to meet your goals.
The first thing you need to do in this instance is to sit with your spouse and discuss in detail what needs to be spent money on. And you agree on each item on this list, write it down and set a timeline for the execution of the plan. When deciding on this, factor in all your income and earnings monthly (for both of you). Eliminate unnecessary spending and debts. If need be, adjust how much will be going into your savings account at the end of each month. This will let you know how much is available for spending and I turn how much can be used for the things you both itemized.

At the end of each month, go to your list and tick the things on the list that have been executed. This will give you an idea of how far you've come and what still needs to be done. As time goes on, you might even see a need to adjust the things on the list. You might need to reprioritize some other things. If you will make a good use of this tool, you must make sure that the things on the list is not entirely your suggestion.

Develop a Financial plan
There are some things at home that require money consistently. In other words those bills are recurrent. Some of those bills are bills for

gas, internet, groceries, and things like that. If your financial goals are to be met, you both need to figure out a way to be paying those recurrent bills every month. Remember, either you are the husband or the wife, you are both involved. With enough cooperation you both will make it work.

Visit your plans weekly
Don't overlook the need for a weekly review of your financial plan. It is true that you already have a plan and there are other financial commitments are already sorted out, you will still need consider how the plan is coming along. A weekly visit will alert you to any distraction that may want to spoil any plans that you have. It will also help you know where to put in more effort. It will help you save more in a case where the current trend might lead to bankruptcy. There are times when you may be awarded a bonus at work. A weekly visit of your financial plan will alert you to where best the bonus should go into.

Hope for the best
There might be times when your plans may falter, don't give up. Unforeseen occurrence can disrupt months and months of plan. Since you are a team, make up for each other when you can. Encourage one another as you move on while commending each other for fulfilling your commitments. Money matters isn't an easy subject among couples so do not fall into the blame game. Criticism will only slow you down while negative comments will only discourage your

partner. When there is a problem with your plans, remember that you are a team. This means that you win together and you lose together.

Let us consider another thing that we all need if our marriages must be successful- hard work.

Chapter Twelve

RULE NO. 16- BE HARDWORKING

Every good thing requires a level of hard work. Marriage is like a fine wheel that needs to be steered continuously to keep it going. It requires effort to make a marriage work out well, in fact, all the vital areas of marriage requires a measure of work. A successful marriage is not a product of chance but a conscientious effort.

Let us briefly consider how effort is needed in some vital areas of marriage.

Responsibilities

The man is the head of the family, and as such he is primarily responsible for the upkeep of the family. Food, shelter, and clothing is your responsibility so to speak even though your wife can assist you. So, as long as you continue to fulfill your responsibilities consistently, there won't be any issues. But fulfilling such tasks cannot just come easy as you might need to be a hardworking man at work and at home. Think for a moment what you think might happen if a husband deliberately stops fulfilling his responsibilities? He may start giving some flimsy excuses and before long, the wife will start getting angry irked up with the new attitude. So yes, in the part of the husband, hard work is required in order to do his job.

A wife is like a support system for the husband. Even though she is not the head of the family, she still plays a very important role in the family. She is responsible for most of the chores at home, cooking, doing groceries and caring for the home. Now for most women, they have their careers as well. Combining all these is definitely not an easy thing to do. For her to keep the wheel rolling, she must be a hard-working woman to fulfill her responsibility. Think too of what might happen if she leaves her responsibilities to chance. Well, the same thing will happen: the peace of the marriage will be threatened.

So, if the marriage is to be successful, enough effort must be put into fulfilling the responsibilities assigned to them.

Communication

Communication between couples should be the most important conversation of all conversations. But the busy lifestyle led by many marriage mates is also threatening this beautiful tool that can cement the bonds between couples. Spouses depart as early as possible for work these days because they need to provide for their needs. But in spite of this challenge, with the right effort, they can still make good use of the available means of communication.

Mobile phones can come in very handy in such situations, but without any effort to put a call through, even this means of communication will still be useless. So, for both the man and the woman, they must both be hardworking if they are to keep in touch throughout the day over the phone while they are both busy at work.

It will also require hard work to spend some time in the evenings with each other after a stressful day at work.

Forgiveness

Earlier in this book, we discussed a very important ingredient necessary for a successful marriage. That ingredient is forgiveness, which means putting up with the mistakes of your spouse and letting the hurt they caused you to go. Well, that too is never going to be possible without effort or hard work. After so many mistakes from the same person, it sure takes a lot of courage to be able to let hurt feelings go. Being patient with your spouse is sure a real working formula for a successful marriage but without any effort, patience cannot be achieved.

Resolving differences- More often than not, you will have some disagreement with your marriage mate. In fact, you will have most of your fights, quarrel and yelling out with them. But, leaving everything to chance will not benefit you both if you are to keep up the same energy that got you together throughout the marriage. You need to resolve your issues as they come up so that there won't be any emotional distance. But the thing is resolving marital issues requires some patience, courage, humility, and hard work. For instance, after a perceived strain your relationship it isn't an easy thing to stand up to go meet your partner and tell them you are sorry even when you know that they are the responsible party for the issue on ground and that they are the ones needing to say they are sorry.

But, its marriage and from time to time you will need to make such allowance for them.

Staying Faithful

If there is a part of marriage that requires hard work it is staying loyal to your marital vows. With the pressure to start an affair whether at work or somewhere else getting greater and greater, it is becoming all the more difficult for both the husband and the wife to stay faithful. True, you will always see someone that is better looking than your spouse, someone richer, with more privileges, and so on. So, staying with that one person is even challenging. But with the proper motivation and the right amount of effort, it is a challenge that can be surmounted. For example, imagine a very attractive workmate at work who is showing extraordinary interest in a married man or woman. As attractive as the workmate might be, they may even be more caring and richer. As attractive they may be, it will surely take a whole new level of hard work and effort for the marriage workmate to be able to fend off such misplaced romantic interest.

Benefits of hard work in a marriage

A better relationship- when you are ready to give your marriage whatever it takes, when you're really hardworking, you will find out that the relationship you enjoy with your spouse, the friendship you have with them will only grow. This is because they will love you for who you are and what you do. They know that you will make any adjustments just to make your marriage work out. This will also make them respect you more. And remember that love and respect are two main ingredients in a marriage.

Happier lives- When you enjoy a healthy relationship with your marriage mate, you will be happy. You see, happiness is a product of hard work, and when you can do what it takes, you will see the results of your hard work. For your marriage to be called a success, joy and happiness must be evident not just to you both but also to outsiders.

Better Health- Will you want to live for as long as you want? The antidote is good health. But how can hard work give you better health? The relationship enjoyed by a husband and his wife is really a special one in which their state of health is determined by how healthy their relationship is. When you both put effort into making each other happy, when you stay faithful to each other even under immense pressure, you will definitely feel comfortable with your spouse anytime you are around them this comfort will translate to a better health condition.

Improved Trust- when you work hard to stay faithful for example, your partner's trust in you will improve. They will be absolutely sure that in spite of external pressure, they always have your back. They will not be insecure because of the new secretary at work or the overly kind neighbor. As the trust between you grow, so does the love you both share.

Cooperation- remember that marriage is teamwork as discussed above. Well, your partner will only be ready to cooperate with you if they too are sure that you are doing your part. Let us explain this point using responsibilities that both the husband and the wife have at home. The man is the head of the family while the woman is the support or complement. Each will keep fulfilling their responsibility if they notice the effort the other is putting into fulfilling theirs. Imagine if one is too lax about their chores, how it will discourage the other partner from doing all they can to keep up with theirs. So the more both parties work hard for this, the more cooperation they will exhibit.

Even though marriage requires a measure of discipline and hard work from both parties, it is really worth the effort. If something is really important to you, you will not feel deterred by how much you need to do to maintain it. Your marriage is going to be successful in the long run. And not just success, it gives both of your lives real value. It strengthens your determination to stay together, it affects how your colleagues view you, and it gives a fitting example to younger ones contemplating marriage. More than all the benefits mentioned, it makes you both happy and contributes immensely to the success of your marriage

RULE NO. 17- KINDNESS

There are many definitions people give kindness to today. It connotes a generous spirit, a caring attitude towards one's spouse, and a feeling of compassion in words and deeds. No doubt this quality is very essential in a successful marriage. For the definition above, kindness is evident not in what we say alone but also in what we do.

Kindness is actually going to be evident in virtually all aspects of the relationship. Let us consider a few areas. But before we do that, let us consider a question that has troubled many for ages.

Is Kindness a Weakness?
People take pride in being strong and stubborn today, especially when men and women brag about their prowess in their marriage. People that are kind are considered old fashioned and weak by their friends and family. Statements like "you are the man of your home" and "I know I'm wrong but will never apologize" are all too common in our society today. This kind of thinking has led many to view kind spouses as weak today.

Kindness as weakness is a misconception that has generated so many enthusiasts. But have you ever asked yourself if kindness isn't how it is painted today? What if kindness is a strength and never a weakness? Can you remember the last time you did something nice for your spouse? It could be a gift that you bought or a sincere commendation that was offered. Ask yourself, 'how did that make them feel'? Can you remember the last time you sincerely told your husband that you were sorry for something you did? Was he not happy at hearing you say that?

Compare that to the last time you castigated or criticized your marriage mate for something said or done. Were they happier after the conversation? Hardly! With that said, it is clear being critical and harsh in dealing with people is a way better approach than treating them unkindly.

Being kind in dealing with your spouse also has a better way of impacting your spouse's mood and attitude. Imagine how being unkind will affect the conversations you may be having subsequently, how it will affect how you both will care for your chores. Definitely, it will be different from how it should be.

If kindness is a weakness, the results of kindness should have been one disadvantage to another. But when things are done in a kind manner, you will find out that the results are more positive. Hence, you will understand that kindness, as opposed to what you may have known or been told is never a weakness but a strength. With that said, let us now consider some practical examples of how to be kind in your marriage.

Kindness in Resolving Differences

There will always be issues to resolve because no one else will piss you off more often than your marriage mate. So, it is very important that you should be kind when resolving such issues. Kindness is first needed when your marriage mate is explaining their side of the story. When they are speaking, the best thing you can do is listen. Now the idea of listening isn't using your mobile phone while they are talking to you. But, really listen. Try to get their side of the story and their point of view. When they feel that you are really listening, then you will be taking the first step in resolving that issue. So as you can see kindness is very vital if you are to successfully resolve your issues as a couple.

Another area where you need kindness when resolving issues is when you are pointing out what your spouse did that was wrong. The way you say those things can either make them happy to apologize or disgruntled. Avoid statements like "It is your fault" or "You never listen to me". Why not replace those statements with things like "How do you think things would have turned out if we did it this way"? Now, the second statement is aimed at triggering the reasoning of your spouse. Without you mandating them, they will be forced to think of what they can do better next time. So, kindness is not apportioning blame but helping your spouse reason on how to be better without you mandating them to be. You see, being kind is a better way of resolving issues than being harsh.

It will also be a sign of kindness to be able to admit that you are wrong, where you need to admit them. Deep down, an offender knows that they have done something wrong. When resolving issues, be determined to be kind by being quick to say you are sorry when you really need to say them.

Imagine how the thing would have turned out if a marriage mate is never kind, never admits their faults even when it is clear that they are at fault, never listens to their spouse when they are pouring out their feeling when they are talking, they always blame their marriage mate in a harsh manner. Such a marriage will be nothing but a disgrace and an unhappy one. Surely, being kind is the only way to resolving an issue.

Kindness in Caring for them
Throughout your time together as a couple, you will need to care for one another consistently. When you care for someone, you will be keenly interested in their well-being. Care is expressed in actions and not in words of mouth. So, being kind will help you understand the real needs of your spouse and will motivate you to do something about it. For example, if you notice that your wife needs a new gas cooker at home and that the current one you now have is giving her some issues, what would be kind move you as a husband to do? If you can afford another one comfortable, wouldn't you buy it for her? If she is ill and can't perform some chores at home like cooking and maybe cleaning the home, what would kindness make a husband do? Nothing stops you from taking care of the home while she is down, knowing full well that the home belongs to both of you.

As a wife, what happens if something happens and your husband is out of a job? Being out of a job means no money to bring home, yet the bills are mounting. If you have the money, kindness will move you to cover for your husband in these trying times. You see, kindness is just going to make you care for your marriage mate in these areas without complaining.

Kindness in dealing with in-laws
Your in-laws are a constant feature of your life from the day you got married. It means from that time on, you will be dealing with them either directly or indirectly. Since the way you relate with them can affect the relationship between you and your marriage mate, it is very important for you to be kind to them as well. There are times that

they might need your help, especially your mate's parents. They will expect you to do one or two things for them. For instance, if you are a husband and your wife's parents are advanced in years there may be certain things that require your direct interference like claiming retirement's benefits and other social benefits if there are any available for older ones in your country. Another example is if you are a wife and your mate's parents don't live very far away from you. They may need to get some house chores done and your husband might not be too available to cater to them. Being kind to your spouse extends to being kind to your in-laws as well. Another area that you need to be kind to your in-laws is when you speak about them to people. It is unkind if you use very derogatory terms in describing them, even if they did something wrong.

Kindness in commendation

The value of commendation cannot be overemphasized. When you are really grateful for things done to you and you show such appreciation in words, you will find out that it will strengthen the relationship between you two. A simple 'thank you' can go a long way in letting them know you are really grateful for what was done. And when you want a favor from them, it will cost you nothing to say 'please' before telling them what you want to be done. You will be surprised at how much this will boost the friendship you both enjoy. When you learn to say those two magic words: 'please' and 'thank you', it is a kind act from you. Kindness will also mean that you refrain from using sarcastic comments when trying to give such commendation.

Kindness in sexual intimacy

This aspect really demands kindness as putting yourself in the place of others will help you deal with them kindly. For example, there are times when things are not so comfy for you your mate and they will naturally not feel inclined to be intimate with them. If your marriage mate is not having a good day, chances are that they may not be too keen on being clingy and sexual. Being kind means understanding them and what they might be going through. When a woman is having her 'monthly visitor', she will be at her lowest during those times. She will be moody, temperamental, and anxious. You will agree that sex and being intimate isn't what they need at that time. They need care and lots of rest. Kindness on your part will make you refrain from pushing for or demanding sexual intercourse during these times.

When you both are making love to each other, kindness will also move you to not demand too much from them as you understand their strength. In fact, kindness will mean not being selfish when trying to satisfy yourself. Kindness will also mean that you don't start talking about the details of sexual intimacy between you and your mate to your friends. That can be embarrassing if your partner finds out.

Kindness is being selfless

Kindness eliminates any trace of selfishness. It motivates one to always want to do something for others, always wanting to make them happy, even at the expense of personal comfort. A kind marriage mate will not be too busy to attend to their spouse. It could be after a very long day at work and they need to talk to you about something that is very much important to them. Even though you are very busy, will you be kind enough to deprive yourself of a few minutes of rest for them? Yes, that is what a kind person will always do. Don't ever let your partner think that work or any other responsibility is more important to you than they are.

Kindness is being generous
This is the most obvious sign your marriage mate will see that will suggest your kindness to them. In fact, some scholars equate kindness with generosity. When you are kind, you take into consideration what they feeling of your spouse are and you offer the help you can to protect them from harm. You thus display a genuine feeling of empathy and affection.

They say kindness is a virtue. It is a quality that drives people to behave well whether they are seen or unseen by others. A kind person will always try to be good to others (your spouse in this respect) without any kind of compensation from them. If you are kind to your spouse, you will always treat them the same way you will want to be treated.

Kindness is shown in the willingness to perform simple acts of favor for your marriage mate like helping out with the dishes or clearing the dinning after a meal together. When you see your spouse in need, and you are in a position to assist them, you will not hesitate to do it. You won't need to be prompted and these kind acts will be done even randomly.

A kind person will naturally be generous. He or she will always be willing to help their spouse with any chore or even give them money for certain things without being asked. Kindness is also evident in your willingness to give of your time to your spouse freely. A kind husband or wife always thinks of their spouse first and what they can do to help them be happy. They thus create a happy environment for them self and their entire household.

Kindness as expressed in assisting others is a virtue that you as a married man or woman should cultivate if you want your marriage to be successful. Be determined to go out of your comfort zone to assist your partner in however little way you can. Try as much as possible to balance up your generosity and your kindness though. Don't fall into the category of people who like to be generous to people outside but are not toward your husband or wife. Remember that they must come first.

Do you remember the golden rule? Just as you want men to do to you so you must do to them. So always imagine what you will like done to you. This will enable you to do the same to your spouse in times of need.

When your wife or husband falls ill, can you try to perform some of their responsibilities? Can you choose to run errands for them, help with their laundry, or buy them some medicines? In fact, you are your mate's doctor, father, mother, friend, and every other thing you can think of. Make sure you cover for them when you can and this will make you the kindest spouse ever.

Genuinely ask your partner how they are after a long day at work. When you ask, really mean it and pay attention when they are responding to that question. That will tell your partner that you really care about them. Make it your aim to always compliment or commend them. A kind person always makes others proud of themselves. Instead of tearing them down with your words during a quarrel, refrain from saying something that will be really damaging to their personality. When you help out with a chore, expect nothing in return.

Always be friendly in disposition and in attitude. Don't be too cold when you are with your partner. It is part of what you can do to be kind to them. Avoid being overly judgmental and quarrelsome. Here is the reality of things, the more kind you are to them, they closer they will be to you and the happier you both will be.

Kindness in avoiding hurtful speech
If you are being kind to your mate, you will not seize every opportunity to take a dig at them, either in public or in private. Now, let us briefly consider the issue of kindness in speaking calmly and respectfully to your spouse. You don't need to start unleashing insults at your partner every time you both disagree on something. Do not let the screaming and yelling be the 'normal thing' in your marriage.

If this is what you experience on a daily basis, determine today that you will put an end to it. One way you can do this is to identify the causes of those sagas and meditate on the importance of adjusting.

Let us consider some reasons why hurtful speech is common in marriages today.

Family upbringing- when children that grow up in a hostile environment where the hurling of insults is prevalent have families of their own, they tend to model their activities after those of their parents that raised them. This is a leading cause of hurtful speech in many marriages.

The Entertainment industry- movies and music videos make hurtful speeches sound like a normal thing that should be used in everyday conversations today. This is evident in what kids say at school on a daily basis. When these kids grow up to have a family of their own, they may think hurling abuses at their spouses in normal.

Culture- In some cultures, all they are taught is that a man must 'be a man'. In other words, when a man is domineering or a commander at home, he is just fulfilling his responsibility. Some cultures are also taught that a woman is only useful for satisfying a man sexually. They make men abuse their wives and hurling insults at their wives becomes something normal to them.

There may be other causes, but whatever it may be; hurtful speech can lead to the end of your marriage if you don't put an end to it. Your words can be as powerful as your fists. That is why verbal abuse is as serious as physical abuse. It can make your spouse fell worthless and unimportant. Worse still, it can make your partner confide in someone else, which will be detrimental to the relationship between you two.

Will you want to be kind to your mate in how you talk to them?

How to conquer hurtful speeches

Be Compassionate

Before you say something to your partner in anger, pause for a moment and ask yourself if you will like the same to be said to you. Try to feel the pain in your heart. Then gradually you will come to understand how what you say always make them feel about themselves. Ask your partner how they will rate you in such instance and what you can do to improve. Avoid justifying what you said as either right or wrong. The most important thing is how what you said made them feel. Then, think of a less hurtful way of expressing your thought.

Imitate Exemplary Couples

There may be some husbands and wife that you appreciate well in your city or religion. They may have been like a role model to you. Why not ask them what helped them overcome the challenge of hurtful speech? Or why not observe how they talk to each other? This can help you to be kind in speech to your marriage mate.

Rekindle Your Feelings

When you were dating and courting, you remember the type of love you both shared back then? The same way you made each other feel was so strong that you won't even think of insulting her by implication let alone insult them by what you said. Try to rekindle such feeling by maybe going out on dates again. You could check on the photos from way back or think about the memories you both shared. These feelings will come back and you will be moved to treat each other with respect again.

Know when to stop

If tempers are beginning to flare and speech is getting out of hand, it might be that since you are both boiling in anger. Why not just stop and allow things to die down before talking about it again. If you want to show more kindness in speech especially when things are quite hot between you two, learn to stop talking when you notice that things are getting out of hand.

So, you can only improve the relationship between you and your spouse by being kind to them.

Chapter Thirteen

RULE NO. 18- SELF-CONTROL

Self-control is the ability to refrain oneself, one's mind, thought or speech from doing something. This is a very important ingredient in a marriage if the marriage will last and be a happy one. A marriage without self-control can be likened to a moving vehicle without properly working brakes. Sooner or later, after a smooth ride it will be very difficult to slow down.

Self-control is important in various aspect of a marriage and it is also a sign the marriage mate that displays it is much matured. Self-control will help you to understand that since you are now part of an immediate family, your wants and desires should now be controlled because what you want as a person must take into consideration what your spouse wants.

Self-control will also make you remember that it is not every time that you have sexual desires that it must be satisfied because what your spouse wants at that moment may be different from what you want, and courtesy demands that you stay kind and consider how they are feeling.

Self –control will also help you remember that even though something is right does not give you the audacity to say them anyhow you want. This is because now you need to start taking into consideration the feelings of your marriage mate. Self-control will also enable you to be faithful in your marriage. There will always be that third party that will aim to threaten the love between you and your wife. Even if this is very tempting, self-control will help you focus your romantic love only on your partner

Strengthening Your Self-Control

If you are the type that struggle with negative feelings, especially sexual feelings or other negative thoughts, examine the things you allow inside of you. Could it be the types of movies you watch? What about the music you listen to? It could also be the books you read or the ways your eyes wander when you see other women. No matter the negative though, be determined never to see a negative image twice. If the first time you see it was by a mistake, try not to take that second glance at it. Reduce the number of romance novels you read. If you are the type that masturbates, be determined to always discuss with your mate when those feelings come and be sure you mate alone satisfies your sexual need.

RULE NO. 19- BE PEACEABLE

Peace is very important in a home. If happiness will thrive, it must start from you both having peace of mind.

Really it doesn't matter who is right or who is wrong, it doesn't matter who the first to apologize is. Only one thing is important- that you take the first step, apologize and make things right. Our little ego will always want to wait for our marriage mate to crawl to us and plead until we are satisfied. But, if you want to really show that you are mature, you need to take the first step and tell your partner how sorry you are- even if you are right. Chances are that they too will be moved to issue an apology for something they did wrong.

As humans, we make some wrong choices and say some hurtful things. When such is brought to the fore, the best thing is to admit out faults and take responsibility for what has happened. A failure to do this will only make your partner very sad and hurt them all the more. No one wants to stay with a partner that never admits when they are wrong. If you are quick to admit your faults, you will quickly be forgiven by your partner.

Being peaceable will also mean that you quickly resolve any issues you may have with your spouse. If you do not resolve those issues on time, they will only get bigger and more difficult to resolve eventually. If care is not taken, you will then need a third party to either come settle it or plead with you both. So the next time you notice there is an issue with your partner promptly call your partner and talk it out with them. Don't let it linger for more than a day.

Remember that you are a team? If you want to overcome challenges to your peace of mind, instead of fighting each other, fight the problem. When you both are together, you are stronger than being apart. So if you are fighting your challenges individually, you are only halving your chances of being successful as a couple.

So, understand that you will hurt each other once in a while and you will say unpleasant things to each other. When this happen, to maintain your peace of mind, you need to pause, and reflect on the goal of a happy marriage that you both share. When you think about this, you will not say something very hurtful. The simple trick is, approach your partner, tell them you're sincerely sorry, and give them a bear hug. If you both are at peace with each other, you will improve your health and overall well-being. Avoid the childish silent treatment while you sit back and wait for your partner to come apologize.

You can also work on yourself if you are to be at peace with each other. If you tend to speak more when you are angry, make sure you pummel yourself to only say things that you mean and won't be so sorry for afterwards. Learn to control your tongue more because when untamed, the tongue can start a war and that will not favor either you or your partner.

If you think your marriage is under attack and peace is something very far away from you right now, you can kindly seek help from a professional or from a trusted religious icon. You can also speak with your parents if you feel comfortable about it. No matter what it takes, make sure to be at peace with your partner.

So in a nutshell, being peaceable goes beyond just not having issues. Even when you do have issues, being peaceable means taking active steps to make peace.

Tips to becoming Peaceful

COMMUNICATION- as we have seen, for a marriage to be really fruitful, the must communicate more. When there is a disappointing situation, we always assume that this is what the other person might be thinking or this is what the other person wanted to do. We make these assumptions without knowing exactly how they feel. We feel entitled all because of the assumption without any credible evidence that we have the truth.

When you have an issue with your spouse, don't just assume as you may be wrong. Ask questions, talk about it so that you can know exactly how they feel instead of assuming you know when in essence you don't know. Remember that you have two different points of view, which needs to be aligned before the issue can be solved. Communication is the only way out of a disagreement and a passport to your peace of mind.

Communication is also pretty important most especially when we have deferring opinions on something. It might be really hard to restart communication. But the faster you start talking after an issue, the easier it is to get over things. A story will suffice here.

There's this couple that had a really big fight, and it resulted in the exchange of words. They both stopped talking to each other and it went on for some days. How then did they manage to live under the same roof? Well, they communicated using notes. The Husband writes notes and puts it on the dining, the wife comes, reads it and replies with a note also.

Well, it went on for quite some time. One a day, the husband comes back home, writes a note and places it on the table. The note reads "I have an interview tomorrow, wake me up by 5 a.m." The wife reads the note, and the next morning when it is 5 a.m., the wife walks to the dining room, writes another note that reads "It's 5 a.m., wake up!"

Well, without being told, you can imagine what would happen to our friend and his wife. The longer you allow communications to suffer, the more your marriage suffers.

FORGIVNESS- In a marriage to be successful, the parties involved must be really good forgivers. When you refrain from extending forgiveness, you are only adding fuel to the fire of discord that may be already on ground you need to let go of the resentment when you receive an apology from your spouse. Some people will only require a series of apologies before they can be placated. This too is very bad a character. It takes great courage to utter the words "I am sorry". Don't make it hard for the person coming to apologize either by setting the stakes so high.

When you forgive your husband or wife for a mistake, do not keep a mental record of it, using it as a weapon for subsequent disagreement. When you forgive them, do so from the depth of your heart and do not bring it up again in the future as if you never forgave them in the first place. There is absolutely nothing like forgiving and forgetting. We were given a memory for a reason, so the advice here when we ask you to forget is -just as we mentioned about- never to use it as a weapon against your mate. Never do that, it hurts.

Forgiveness goes as far as if your mate becomes unfaithful. Yes, and we stand by it. The truth is, couples have a lot more to forgive themselves of than meets the eye. So if your mate gets unfaithful, while you have the option to walk away from that marriage and divorce him or her, always consider the option of forgiveness.

But remember, you own your marriage, if after cheating on you, you feel you can't forgive and want to move on, please consider the costs of both staying and leaving, then make the decision that is best for your own situation.

BE PATIENT- Being patient with your spouse involve never expecting too much from them, too much than they can give. It is really immature to always get annoyed over very little things. And when you want to discuss something with your spouse and they say "can we discuss this later today?" please, be really patient with them, they might have an important thing to attend to at work. If you forget to be patient, it will only led to a situation where every little thing done at home becomes an issue and soon enough there will be one issue after another. If you are wrong too, it will be the right thing if you willingly apologize without any prompt from your husband or wife.

COMPROMISE- At one point or the other, you will have to come to a compromise or an understanding with your spouse. Sometimes, the feelings of your spouse might be affected and your feelings too may be affected simultaneously. When these happen, it comes down to letting things go and you both coming to an agreed understanding. There are some traits that your partner process that you may never be able to change. Since there is nothing you can really do about them, you will need to learn how to live with them like that. That right there is a reasonable compromise. If you don't, you will just find yourself complaining about every little thing in the home and that will only take the peace away from your relationship. Think about it too that even you have some traits that your partner has no other option but to manage.

It is very important that you figure what these traits may be during courtship, and better understand your partner for who they are. While some traits can be managed, others might be very hard to manage, and you might have pretty strong views about these. Long before marriage is the time to find these traits and see if you'll be able to live with them or not.

While you might be able to live with your partner, always remember, that you can rarely ever change others. You can testify to just how hard it is for you to make some changes in the way you do things, so be very careful of how much of a compromise you'll be willing to take before you agree to walk into that marriage.

A man or woman who hits you before marriage, even if it is after losing their temper could become even more physically abusive after marriage. So while we encourage compromise, never give off too much that you'll lose your identity.

TRUST- If you want peace at home, you must try hard to trust your marriage mate. Checking their mobile phones and messages always, nagging over trivial things and questioning their every move will only cause occasional issues between you two. If they have never really given you a cause to not trust them, don't start suspecting their intentions for doing one thing. If you start questioning and monitoring them, they might lose the respect they have for you, and there will be one more thing to argue about daily. This will not contribute to the happiness and success of your marriage. When they make calls, stop asking them who that was every time. Don't encroach on their privacy or their personal space.

RESPECT- When you give your spouse some respect; you get respected back in return. If you habitually disrespect your husband or wife, you just can't expect them to keep respecting you. You only get what you give. So if you want problems to be few in your marriage, learn to respect your spouse. When in the middle of an argument, try not to say things that will humiliate your spouse. When you both are in public places, try to accord them some measure of respect as this will send a clear signal to anyone watching that you respect your husband or wife. On the other hand, if you don't respect your spouse in public, you are only giving others a license to disrespect them.

RESOLVE THE ISSUE- As a general rule, don't mix the problems of yesterday with that of today. That means if there is an issue; don't leave it unresolved before going to bed. Try to discuss it and be happy with each other. If your partner is not opposed to it, in cases where the matter isn't easily resolved, try to make some hot and passionate love to bed. Chances are that when you both wake up the next day, you will both be in a better position to talk it out amicably.

GET HELP-

In some rare cases, a disagreement may be too cumbersome to be resolved over a one-on-one discussion. In such cases, you can involve a third party, which could be a professional. The help may also be your parents or your in-laws. They can come in really handy when you've tried all other options in resolving the issue.

There is no success in a marriage if the parties involved are not at peace with each other. Now, we proceed to the final rule, one that many overlook today. That is being of the same mind when it comes to parenting.

RULE NO. 20- PROPER VIEW OF PARENTING

There are many reasons why couples disagree today, some disagree over sexual intimacy, others over the number of children they should have, others over money, they type of marriages they should have, and so on. However, there is one crucial topic that always causes problems in the home- parenting. Issues over the proper way to raise kids have been found to affect the atmosphere I the home and the overall success of the marriage.

Before kids show up, a couple might have been the best of friends as well as gist buddies. But when kids arrive, they will be at loggerheads over trivial things like where to live, where they can go, sometimes how much sex they should be having, and so on. Some parents may be stricter than the other, while one may want their kids to be as smart as they are at all costs.

The truth is that most marriage feels the pain when these issues about parenting come up. But think back to when we were kids. We all got some limits that were set for us by our parents. If they could set limits for us and those limits made us better persons today, then it is only normal to set reasonable limits for our children. Without such limits, the whole home will be in a state of anarchy as children will just do as they like. As earlier mentioned, kids don't want limits and parents can differ on the amount of limits that must be set for kids.

How to Reason on Child Limits

Dialogue

When you start having kids, it is good that you and your partner start discussing the strategies that you both will employ when the kids grow up to that state where they need some measure of limits. Start this kind of discussion well in advance. Don't be too keen on making your desires stick. Allow your partner talk about their own ideas too, and then you both can decide on which strategy will work best for you. Since you both will not always want the same thing, be prepared to compromise in some areas.

Mutual Agreement

When setting house rules, make sure it is what you and you marriage mate agrees on. Sit down to talk about why you are making such rule in case you have kids. For safekeeping, write them down. This will help you not to forget those things. Some of the things you can agree on is how much time you will allow your child watch television, what time you want them to sleep daily, and so on.

When your kids are of age, promptly let them know each house rules and tell them the consequences of not complying.

Mutually agree on consequences

When house rules are broken, there will always be consequences. As parents, there might be different ideas of punishment in their head. Some parents might favor some spanking while others might prefer grounding. So that these conflicting ideas don't start causing some issues, it is best to agree on them before conflicting ideas start causing some issues. Some parents might decide that some form of punishment might be too harsh for some kids to handle. So, just as you want to make a list of house rules, you can also make a list of the consequences of breaking each house rule.

Have each other's back

The plan is already in place, the right thing to do is both stand on the same level by having each other's back when it is time to implement them. Never let any child make you and your spouse abandon what you have prepared for them. When one parent is lenient, overriding the rule while the other is trying to stick with the rule, it will only cause a palpable discord between you both. It will also tell the kids that you are not serious with any other rules you give them.

Never Argue in front of your children over the rules

You and your wife will only become a laughing stock for your kids if you do this. So, when one of you is administering the discipline, refrain from interfering. The picture it will paint in the minds of your children if you start arguing in front of them will only put you parents at a disadvantage. Children can easily notice when their parents are not in agreement. As long as your partner isn't overly abusive, let them administer the consequence.

Even if you are not comfy with how the discipline was administered, privately let your partner know this instead of doing it in front of the kids.

Be Adaptable

As your children grow older, you might see a need to adjust some rules to fit their present age and circumstances. When this happen, don't be too rigid. Make the needed adjustment. Of course the adjustment should not be made unilaterally.

KEY POINTS

- Don't fight your spouse in front of your kids

- Support each other in front of your kids even if you feel something is not right

- Self-control is needed to remain faithful to your spouse.

Conclusion

As we have seen, marriage is a very beautiful institution that can benefit both the parties involved: the husband and the wife. Sadly, most marriages today only head in one direction- divorce. The rate at which this is getting higher and higher is alarming, even to marriage experts. Among celebrities, divorce is nothing new to them as some have even divorced more than once.

This does not mean that marriages will never succeed. There are couples that have enjoyed decades together as marriage mates, and are still waxing stronger. What is the difference? A strong determination to make things work out between them. As earlier opined in this book, every good thing needs a measure of effort. We can think of it this way: for a dish to be delicious, it must be well garnished with all the vital ingredients that will contribute to the overall taste. In the same vein, for a marriage to be successful, those involved must display the necessary qualities highlighted in this book.

No matter how much you display the needed qualities; there will still be times when things may falter. We are not promising a perfect life. You are both imperfect and will probably remain as that. But when you strive to apply the suggestions in this book, problems will be few. There will not be any cause for a dispute that can't be reconciled.

Yes, your marriage can be successful against all odds.

References

www.jw.org

Book- 5 Love Languages (Gary Chapman)

Book- The 7 Principles for Making Marriage Work (John Gottman)

www.ingramcontent.com/pod-product-compliance
Lightning Source LLC
Chambersburg PA
CBHW071519080526
44588CB00011B/1490